The End of the Beginning

Bracknell Paper No. 3
A Symposium on the Land/Air Co-operation in the Mediterranean War 1940-43

20 March 1992

Sponsored jointly by the Royal Air Force Historical Society and the Royal Air Force Staff College Bracknell

Copyright © 1992 by Royal Air Force Historical Society

First published in the UK in 1992

ISBN 0951982419

All rights reserved. No part of this book may be reproduced or transmitted in any form or by any means, electronic or mechanical including photocopying, recording or by any information storage and retrieval system, without permission from the Publisher in writing.

Printed by Hastings Printing Company Limited

Royal Air Force Historical Society

Contents

Preface

Quotations

1. Opening Remarks:
   Air Commodore R.H. Gould
2. Chairman's Introduction: Air Chief Marshal Sir Michael Armitage
3. Land/Air Co-operation: Mr. John Terraine
4. The Shape and Course of the Mediterranean War:
   Major General John Strawson
5. The RAF in the Mediterranean Theatre: Mr. Humphrey Wynn
6. How the Joint System Worked: (i) Sir Frederick Rosier and (ii) Sir Kenneth Cross
7. The Commanders and the Command System:
   Dr. Vincent Orange
8. Digest of Group Discussions: A to G
9. Closing Address: Air Chief Marshal Sir Michael Armitage
10. Closing Remarks by the Deputy Commandant Air Commodore Gould and the Chairman of the RAF Historical Society Air Marshal Sir Frederick Sowrey
    Biographical Notes on the Main Speakers
    The Royal Air Force Historical Society
    Acknowledgement

Senior Air Commanders

Air Chief Marshal
Sir Arthur Tedder

Air Vice Marshal
Coningham

Acting Air Commodore
Harry Broadhurst

Preface

Land/Air Co-operation in the Mediterranean War 1940-43 is the title of the third of the on-going series of seminars entitled the Bracknell Papers. The seminar was convened jointly by the RAF Historical Society and the RAF Staff College on 20th March 1992 at Bracknell.

The capacity audience consisted of members of the RAF Historical Association and the Bracknell Directing staff and students.

Contributions were made by former RAF and Army officers, including historians with a variety of origins.

The day's proceedings were presided over by Air Chief Marshal Sir Michael Armitage and a similar pattern to the two previous symposia was maintained.

The morning was devoted to a series of six talks on various campaign aspects, while in the afternoon the symposium was divided into discussion groups in which issues raised were debated in more detail. These provided an opportunity for Middle East veterans and others to offer recollections and for historians to comment further on a variety of questions and controversies.

The volume contains the edited texts of the main talks and a digest of what was said in the discussion groups.

Derek Wood
Editor

"It is not the end. It is not even the beginning of the end. But it is perhaps the end of the beginning."

Winston S. Churchill
10th November 1942

Speech to the House of Commons on the victory at El Alamein.

"The main thing with air superiority is not only getting it but even more important knowing when you have it."

A desert air commander 1942
Air Chief Marshal Sir Harry Broadhurst

"The lesson that I have learnt today is that there are no new lessons to be learnt, only lessons to be remembered."

A staff college student 1992
Squadron Leader A. J. Stewart

1. Opening Remarks

The Deputy Commandant
Air Commodore R. H. Gould

It is my great pleasure to welcome you on behalf of the Commandant. This is the third such seminar that we have co-hosted at Bracknell with the RAF Historical Society. Two years ago the subject was the Battle of Britain; the day was enormously successful and proved the value of the joint forum of historians, those who had fought in the campaign, and current members of the RAF Historical Society and the Advanced Staff Course. Last year the subject was the Battle of the Atlantic and it comes as no surprise to me as a maritime aviator that somewhat fewer lessons could be learned in this esoteric and by now highly formalised area of joint military endeavour. Today we return to more fertile ground in our study of the Mediterranean war. This was where many of the lessons of joint land/air operations were learned and sometimes re-learned for application in other campaigns both during World War II and subsequently. Most recently many members of the Advanced Staff Course and the RAF Historical Society contributed to operations Granby and Desert Storm and I feel confident they will play a full role in to-day's proceedings, perhaps offering the historians and old campaigners some new perspectives on joint warfare. Without further ado and in anticipation of a fascinating and memorable day, may I now hand over to your Chairman for the day Air Chief Marshal Sir Michael Armitage.

2. Chairman's Introduction

Air Chief Marshal
Sir Michael Armitage, KCB, CBE

Our first speaker is one of the most distinguished - if not the most distinguished - military historians in this country today, John Terraine. I first came across his writings in his ten books about the First World War and his five or so other books on a variety of military topics. He became well known to a much wider public through his many contributions to television programmes on military history and not least that famous series on the Great War. But he is perhaps best known to this audience for his works on the U-boat wars and above all for that classic of RAF history, The Right of the Line.

As you will hear from John, air power played a vital part in operations on the Western Front in the First World War but not in what we would now call direct support of the armies. Contrary to popular belief the dominant weapon in that conflict was not the machine gun but the artillery piece and it was largely in support of those weapons during the trench warfare of that conflict that land/air co-operation first developed. The Second World War was not about trench warfare and it was therefore not about air support for artillery. John is going to talk about those changes and where they left us by the end of 1940.

3. Land/Air Co-operation

Mr John Terraine

The Gospel tell us, "In the beginning was the Word . . . and the Word was God." That is a gratifying message for historians, and helpful to one and all inasmuch as it leads one to look for key words in a variety of subjects. I am here today to tell you that in the beginning of Air Power was Co-operation — but alas! the word got somewhat garbled in the gospels of the Royal Air Force.

It is my task now to take us back to the beginning of the subject, which is (for us) exactly 80 years ago. In *January 1912* a newly-formed Air Committee was discussing the formation of a *British Aeronautical Service,* and the chairman of its technical sub-committee, Colonel J. E. B. Seely, said at one of its meetings,

> "At the present time in this country we have, as far as I know, of actually flying men in the Army about eleven, and of actual flying men in the Navy about eight, and France has about two hundred and sixty-three, so we are what you might call behind."

As it turned out, this was not a bad thing to be — but I would hesitate to offer the lesson that being behind is *necessarily* a good thing.

They moved pretty fast in 1912; a *Royal Flying Corps* was quickly formed, and it received a *Royal Warrant on April 12;* it had an Army Wing and a Navy Wing and a Central Flying School. On *July 1 1914* the Naval Wing separated off to form the *Royal Naval Air Service under the Admiralty,* and that was how the Air Services went to war a month later — as parts of the Navy and of the Army. So there wasn't much doubt that there would be some degree of co-operation between Air and Sea, and Air and Land.

When war came, in *August 1914,* the Royal Flying Corps had no fewer than 179 aircraft on its books, but we should not become over-excited by that figure. What rather spoils its impact is the fact that quite a few of them wouldn't really fly, and quite a few more wouldn't fly very well; so it was only with difficulty that the RFC put four squadrons into the air with 12 aircraft each on initial establishment.

Just to fill the picture, our *French* allies were credited with 136 *serviceable* aircraft, and the *Germans* could put up about 180, as well as 9 Army airships — the famous Zeppelins.

The question then promptly arose; what did all this new aerial armament exist for? How was it to be used? As regards France and Britain, the answer is supplied by two pre-war annual *Army manoeuvres, in 1911 and 1912*.

In the *French* manoeuvres in 1911, air reconnaissance *in conjunction with cavalry* was tried, but not very much is said about it; it certainly doesn't sound very promising. The significant feature of the French exercises was *air co-operation with artillery*, and according to British observers even at that early date the progress made was impressive.

The essence of this technique, then as ever more, was *communication* — communication between the flying machine in the sky and the batteries on the ground; no easy matter in 1911, nor for many years afterwards. The French tried out various forms of *signalling*, both direct and via captive balloons — that must have been something worth watching — and by *wireless telegraphy*. It was probably pretty clear even then that this was the real way forward, but we have to remember that for a long time what it meant was tapping out Morse from a cumbersome transmitter in a very small, cramped aeroplane cockpit with one hand, while trying to fly the thing with the other.

Very simple things can work wonders, but they all have to have a beginning — someone has to think of them. For *air-to-ground fire control*, the stark essential is *squared maps*, and it appears that the French were actually using such maps in the 1911 manoeuvres. In fact, the British Official Air Historian said:

"In short, almost all the uses which later became commonplace of the war were exemplified in the French manoeuvres of 1911."

"*Almost* all"; one use which was obviously not practiced was *combat*. That proved to be an inevitable adjunct of the artillery co-operation which was very clearly seen to be an aircraft rôle, and it is difficult to exaggerate their joint importance in both the world wars of this century.

The second important rôle was displayed with great effect in the *British* manoeuvre of 1912. The opposing commanders were Generals Sir Douglas Haig and Sir James Grierson, the brightest rising stars of Haldane's new-style Army. Each side had a squadron of 7 aeroplanes and an airship. Haig's airship, the *Delta*, broke down, but Grierson's, the *Gamma*, supplied what the Official Air History calls

"the *first triumph of aerial reconnaissance* in England."

Basing his plans on this, Grierson was the clear winner. He said in his report

"The airship, as long as she remained afloat, was of more use to me for strategical reconnaissance than the aeroplanes, as being *fitted with wireless telegraphy,* I received her messages *in a continuous stream and immediately after the observations* had been made."

What more could a general ask? Grierson was duly grateful, and he paid this tribute to his air contingent:

"The impression left on my mind is that their use has *revolutionised the art of war."*

Lecturing to the Royal Artillery Institution the following year, he went even further; "personally," he said,

"I think there is no doubt that before land fighting takes place, we shall have to *fight the enemy's aircraft* . . . warfare will be impossible unless we have the *mastery of the air."*

And that, of course, was precisely what transpired; it would not be long before command of the air was regarded as a prime ingredient of land battle.

In August 1914 Haig and Grierson were the two Army Corps commanders of the original Expeditionary Force. Unfortunately, Grierson died of a heart attack before a shot was fired, but Haig never forgot the lesson he had learned in 1912. We have a vivid picture of him reacting instantly to an airman's report during the retreat from Mons, and from the very beginning he paid the closest attention to what was revealed by the new "eye in the sky".

The French, on the other hand, by August 1914 had lost interest in strategic reconnaissance. They had *a Plan,* which they intended to carry out come what may, and the value of aircraft was judged by what they could *contribute to the fulfilment* of that plan, not to making changes in it. It seems unbelievable, but it is a simple fact that the French Air Service completely missed the great swing of the German right wing — a mass of manoeuvre of over a million men — through Belgium and Northern France. The reason why the French missed this unconcealable spectacle was very simple: their aircraft were in the wrong place, looking the wrong way — towards Lorraine and Alsace, as dictated by the Plan, not Luxembourg and Belgium, as dictated by the *German* plan.

The Germans themselves were even worse. General Staff thinking fully accepted the "fog of war", and believed that *"an energetic offensive replaced accurate information."* They considered that they did not *need* air reconnaissance and they did not want it.

They even held that too much information was liable to *weaken a commander's resolve* just when he might be needing it most. This now seems a fairly amazing view.

So they missed the arrival of the BEF in France, they missed its presence at Mons until they actually bumped into it, they lost it for most of the retreat from Mons, and they completely missed the regrouping of the French Army for the Battle of the Marne.

The RFC, by contrast, didn't miss much. It seized the reconnaissance rôle indicated in 1912 unhesitatingly — as far as its equipment (and numbers) allowed.

So the "eye in the sky" was established as the very first contribution of the Air to war, the first aspect of Land/Air Warfare.

And deep reconnaissance was also, of course, the first *strategic rôle* of air forces.

It never ceased to be of the highest value in the First World War; in the Second, it is hard to think of any operations that did not rely on Air Reconnaissance, especially Photographic Reconnaissance or bitterly regret its absence.

Whether done by high-speed hedge-hoppers or by satellites, it can never be a bad thing to see over the hill, and bring back a picture of what you see.

The truth is, of course, that at the very beginning there was not a lot else that the fragile aircraft of the period could do.

All aircraft on both sides were underpowered; aerial bombs had yet to be designed — though you could drop explosives in containers over the side of an open cockpit by hand, hoping for the best. And the first air combats were fought with revolvers.

Tactical reconnaissance, though, was something else again, and tactical reconnaissance in conjunction with artillery became the next prime duty of the airmen.

Once the armies went to ground in the trenches, and these became more and more complex and extensive, the First World War became essentially *an artillery war*.

By that I mean that it was artillery that decided the outcome of battles, artillery that inflicted by far the largest number of casualties, and artillery that put a stamp of brutal destructiveness on the entire proceeding.

Incidentally, the Second World War was also an artillery war, for the same reason

Except in the campaigns which displayed , in various ways, vastly unequal forces "tigers eating tomcats", as the saying goes, once more it was the guns that decided the battles (well supported, let me say at once, by tactical aircraft) and the guns that inflicted most of the casualties on all fronts.

When it came to sheer destruction, however, air bombing undoubtedly took the palm!

Tactical reconnaissance for artillery immediately took two forms which have a look of being eternal; they can perhaps be best expressed as questions:

    where is the target?
    have I hit it?

and as a rider to the second, of course, "where did my shot go?"

Inter-Allied co-operation in 1914 was not all that it might have been; it seems that there was little awareness, as the RFC buckled down to its new task, of what the French had already been devising back in 1911.

The RFC itself had done a small amount of pre-war experimentation with the Royal Artillery — but small is the word, restricted by there being *very few aircraft available* and *very little practice ammunition,* thanks to the Treasury.

So the AFC had to start from scratch which, when you study British military history, sometimes seems to be the national favourite position.

It didn't waste any time. Already by *September 1914* Lieutenant D.S. Lewis(ex-R.E.) had devised a squared map for identifying ground targets, and this very quickly became standard equipment throughout the B.E.F.

In January 1915, with the experience of the First Battle of Ypres to draw upon, an RFC/RA conference was held, at which Captain B.T. James (also ex-R.E.) pointed out that the infantry's musketry procedure, indicating target positions by *clock-face references,* would be just the thing for reporting fall of shot.

Lewis seized on this, and incorporated it in a celluloid disc, which he pinned to his map, with its centre on the target — and scientific spotting took off from there.

By 1917 it had reached the stage of being an essential part of the artillery programme; the gunners felt blind without it.

The Germans by then had developed a nasty habit, when a big battle was impending, of concealing a number of their batteries which would spring to life in unexpected places at zero hour.

It was an RFC function to keep a sharp eye open for these, and report their presence by *"Now Firing" (NF) calls,* so that they could be immediately engaged by counter-battery shoots.

Not being idiots, the Germans were aware of this, and their *wireless listening service* accordingly cocked an ear for the NF calls; as soon as it heard one, the battery in question was notified, and with luck it might just have time to change its position before too much harm was done. But quite often it did not, and the Royal Artillery enjoyed a feast.

When, for one reason or another, but usually weather, this kind of help from the "eye in the sky" was not forthcoming, it was a bad day for the guns, and a bad day for the guns was a bad day indeed for the infantry.

July 31 1917, the first day of the *Third Battle of Ypres,* was such a day.

Visibility was bad, with drizzle turning to heavy rain, making air observation impossible; there were *no* NF calls that day.

As a result, the infantry, having started well, went too far and nobody knew quite where it was; the Germans, as ever, put in a series of counter-attacks; the artillery was helpless, and the infantry had to abandon much of the ground it had won and a lot of the guns it had captured.

By contrast, on September 20, *the Battle of the Menin Road Ridge,* there were 394 air messages, which gave ample warning of every German grouping for counter-attack.

The artillery responded to SOS signals in under half a minute and the Machine Gun Corps in a matter of seconds; every counter-attack was broken up before it was even launched, and if that battle was not a victory we shall have to find a new word.

But the best was yet to come; this time it owed everything to co-operation between the RFC and the *Royal Engineers.*

The first use of *aerial photography for mapping* — first use by the British, that is — was at Neuve Chapelle in March 1915; thereafter this too became a standard part of battle preparation.

But between 1915-17 the RFC took part in a far more elaborate exercise — an aerial survey of the whole of the British front, enabling the Royal Engineers to produce (at last) a really accurate map on the scale of 1:20,000 which was the basis of the "artillery boards" supplied to all the batteries.

This map, and the practice of calibrating every single gun which now became standard drill, made *predicted shooting* possible. And what that meant was, as I have said in my book WHITE HEAT: The New WARFARE 1914-1918 (just republished), that now the artillery

> "could engage precise targets with a reasonable expectation of scoring direct hits or damaging near misses, instead of, in effect, blazing away at a landscape."

Furthermore, it meant that the preliminary registration and the long preliminary bombardments which had advertised all the offensives of previous years were no longer necessary; so when this new method was first tried, at Cambrai on November 20 1917, the 1,003 guns of General Byng's Third Army opened fire at Zero hour with a single crash and no warning at all, and the day was a great success. What it meant was that *Surprise and Precision* were now restored to battle practice, and with the addition of smoke for *Protection,* they are what at last unlocked the trench deadlock in 1918.

This result was a direct fruit of Land/Air Co-operation — in fact its most valuable fruit — and it is one of history's great extraordinary circumstances that it took until 1942 before the penny dropped in the next war, at the Battle of El Alamein.

And there was something else as well that was on the point of bearing fruit at the end of 1942. In the next two years we began to hear what most people (including a good few who should have known better) thought was a new word for a new idea: *interdiction*. It means, very simply, sealing off a battlefield by air power, interdicting the enemy's power to withdraw or reinforce by cutting his communications, choking off his supplies, and thus isolating an area in which the ground forces can bring overwhelming superiority to bear.

The word may have been new; the idea was not. The RFC had first tried it during the Battle of Loos in September 1915. The results were, frankly, pathetic — as one might suppose. The objective was to break up the railway system supplying the German front in the battle area to a distance of about 36 miles behind the line. It was altogether too much for the resources then available. A small amount of damage was done, which is fairly amazing, but there was no check to the flow of German reinforcements and munitions into the area.

There were *too few aircraft* for such an ambitious programme, and the aircraft themselves *did not have the performance* (we should remember that real aerial bombs came late in the day and that the first, distinctly crude, bomb-sight had only just been received on the eve of battle).

It was a familiar story, summed up by the American historian John Cuneo:

"Throughout World War I the air services of all nations — not only the RFC — kept trying to accomplish too much with too little."

It was a *matter of technology*, of performance even more than numbers; and it was never resolved in that war.

At the Battle of Amiens, on August 8 1918, *the "black day" of the Germany Army*, the Allies deployed over 1,900 aircraft: over 1,100 French and some 800 RAF. But for the young RAF, it was also a "black day": attempting interdiction by destroying the bridges over the River Somme behind the German front, it had 45 aircraft shot down and 52 more so badly damaged that they had to be written off.

The bridges stood — thanks in large part to the Fighter arm of the German Air Force. Interdiction would have to wait to produce its intended effect — and there is still doubt about whether it ever really performed all it promised. I think the American experience in Vietnam may throw some harsh light on that subject.

And there was something else, too, that would have to wait.

We saw, with a shudder, what aircraft can perform on the actual battlefield itself in 1940: the German *Stukas* — the Ju 87 dive-bombers — produced an immense effect in the Battle of France. For psychological impact it was not really matched until the Battle of Normandy in 1944, when the *Allied Tactical Air Forces* descended on the German armour and gun positions and transport and shot them to bits.

It was not that nobody had thought of tactical air power between 1914-

18 — on the contrary, they were always trying it. But once again, there was the question of aircraft performance.

The low-speed aircraft of the day were too vulnerable, *their armament too insignificant* to produce much in the way of results, except in special conditions.

One such was the great German advance in March 1918, when suddenly the landscape filled with troops and vehicles out in the open and targets appeared that could make an airman's mouth water.

The British and French flyers had a go, and they certainly produced effects — but these were local, and in relation to the scale of the battle, insignificant.

Now I dare say that you may be thinking that I have spent a disproportionate amount of my time on World War I.

You may also — I certainly hope so — by now be understanding *why*. What, after all have I been talking about? Well, the subjects were:
>strategic reconnaissance,
>tactical reconnaissance,
>photographic reconnaissance,
>aerial survey,
>anti-submarine reconnaissance,
>artillery co-operation,
>interdiction, and
>the tactical use of air.

So what is there left?

In terms of absolute *innovation* — other than the steady improvements of technology (better aircraft, improved communication, better weapons) — the answer is, "very little".

In terms of *system and control* however, the answer becomes — after a time — "a good deal".

What had happened, in the stark words of Sir Maurice Dean, was that
>"Between 1918 and 1939 the RAF forgot how to support the Army."

It was a big thing to forget; and the reason for this forgetfulness, I regret to say, was an intrusion of the very factor that had marred the German and French application of air power in 1914 — *dogma*.

The dogma in question, of course, was the belief in the strategic bomber offensive and the ability of the bombers to deliver a "knock-out blow".

Based on very selective readings of bombing experience in the First War, the bomber dogma remained unmoved by further experiences *between* the wars. It dismissed the very evident fact that several years of a war which included some very lively bombing by the Japanese *did not produce a "knock-out blow" in China*. And spectacular air-raids by

Italian and German aircraft *in Spain*, while evidently causing a lot of damage in Madrid and Barcelona, did not produce a "knock-out blow" there either.

German air intervention on the Spanish *battlefields*, however, did have a very definite effect; the Nationalists won command of the air in 1938, and thereafter the issue of the war was not in doubt.

But the Chief of the Air Staff, Sir Cyril Newall, pronounced this to be "a gross misuse of air forces".

Unrepentant of their heresy, however, the Germans did it again in 1940. In the Battle of France they seized air supremacy and proceeded (as I have said here before) to *saturate the battlefield with air power* — and won the battle hands down, to the dire humiliation of their enemies.

The prime instrument of this success, which really did produce a "knock-out blow" — knocking out a major military power, France, in about six weeks, and reducing Britain to a desperate defensive — was not the bomber, the favoured weapon of the air doctrinaires, but *the fighter*.

In France, in 1940, the fighter was the sanction of all that occurred or did not occur; it was some 1,200 modern fighters that gave Germany *air supremacy*, and with it, victory. And by "fighters" I mean, almost entirely, the Messerschmitt 109.

And here, certainly, was something new, because no aircraft of any type in World War I was able to produce such an effect as that.

The Germans repeated the lesson in 1941, in Greece, and we suffered another humiliating débâcle — all the worse, if anything, because we had just had the pleasure of inflicting one.

In the Libyan Desert, against the Italian Air Force, the RAF's supremacy had been absolute, and General O'Connor was able to plan and carry out his famous Desert Victory virtually without regard to the enemy air force — which was something of a luxury.

When the *Germans* entered the Desert War, such a happy condition never recurred.

Once more we had to *fight for air supremacy* against the German fighter arm — but never of course, on anything like the scale of France in 1940: after June 1941 the bulk of the German Air Force was co-operating with the main body of the German Army in Russia.

However, what there was of it in the Desert was enough to make it a long, hard haul before we, in our turn, could saturate a battlefield with air power.

It was really not until the *Battle of Alam Halfa, in September 1942*, that that time came, and it was our famous enemy, Field-Marshal Rommel, who most clearly expressed its meaning; Rommel said:

"Anyone who has to fight, even with the most modern weapons, against an enemy in complete control of the air fights like a savage against modern European troops, under the same handicaps and with the same chances of success."

You could hardly find a terser, more accurate summary of the object and significance of Land/Air warfare.

It is really extraordinary how many things "came good" for us in 1942 — three years into the war, in most cases spent trying to get back to where we had been in 1918.

The return of predicted shooting and the *systemisation of Army Co-operation* were just two of them.

And the latter was no easy matter, it didn't just happen by sudden inspiration.

After the Fall of France, it was quite clear that something had better be done — and fairly quickly — about Land/Air Warfare; the RAF had to be brought back effectively to the battlefield where it was born.

But the RAF in England had a problem: the functional Commands.

For Operations purposes there were three:
> Bomber Command, whose function was *to carry the war to Germany* — and there was nothing else that could do that;
> Fighter Command, whose prime duty (magnificently performed in the Battle of Britain) was *to protect the United Kingdom;*
> and Coastal Command, ever more deeply engaged in the decisive Battle of the Atlantic, in other words, Sea/Air Co-operation.

Where did Army Support come in?

The RAF's answer — very understandable — was that in relation to the existing Commands, it didn't: so there had better be a new Command precisely for the purpose — *Army Cooperation Command.*

It was plausible — but it wasn't the right answer; frankly, I don't think there *was* a right answer, for the RAF in England.

The only thing I can think of is the adoption of the German system of *Lufftlotte* — *mixed component air fleets;* and a structural transformation of that magnitude in the crisis of a war was simply not a practicality.

The practicality was discovered where you would expect it to be discovered — at the sharp end of the war, which from our point of view was now *the Middle East.*

Middle East Command was not like the others; it did not have a specialised function — other than *being* in the Middle East and doing its fighting there. What I mean by that is that it was not really a Command — it was an Air Force.

The fighting itself required *all types of aircraft:* long-range bombers and short-range bombers, fighters, reconnaissance and "pathfinder" aircraft, transport — the lot.

And it was the particular contribution of Middle East Command, under Lord Tedder, to discover and accept, as I said in THE RIGHT OF THE LINE,
> "that when critical land operations are in progress, army co-operation is not simply a specialised activity of part of an air force. It is the function of *the entire force*, with all its available strength."

That is the real meaning of "saturating a battle area" — and battle areas nowadays go a long way back.

In a crisis — and the Middle East was not often short of these — it meant *interdiction* in various forms by the *heavy bombers*, constant attacks by *mediums* to produce the effect described by Rommel, *fighter-bombers* going for close pin-point targets (such as tanks), *fighters* in their true rôle, covering the whole thing, constant *photo-reconnaissance*, and *transports* for air supply and to evacuate casualties: ie. the *whole force*.

Such was the development of Land/Air Co-operation, as it evolved between 1942-45, and the subject that we shall now proceed to examine in greater depth for the rest of today's seminar.

Chairman

Thank you very much indeed for that indispensable background to our discussions for the rest of the day. So far we have heard about the historical background to the land/air campaign in North Africa and now to give us a feel for the wider issues involved in that campaign I am pleased to welcome a most distinguished soldier, historian and writer, Major General John Strawson. I think it was I who suggested his name for this seminar; like many others here I was familiar with the eleven books he had written or co-authored on military topics; three of them dealing specifically with the war in the Mediterranean theatre. General Strawson had a most distinguished career as a fighting soldier, serving with the 4th Hussars, Churchill's old regiment of course, in this very campaign in North Africa. After the war he took part in many internal security operations and campaigns, including that in Borneo where he commanded his Regiment. Later he commanded an Infantry Brigade, filled other senior appointments and was later Chief of Staff UK Land Forces.

The wider issues on which he has been asked to address us include the German ambitions in the Mediterranean theatre and what that region meant to the Allies. He will talk to use particularly about the offensives and counter-offensives that saw the Armies of both sides advance and retreat along the coast of North Africa, and he will also tell us how the final British Army offensive from El Alamein onwards was supported by the British air forces in the theatre.

4. The Shape and Course of the Mediterranean War 1940-43

Major General John Strawson, CB, OBE

One of the most striking things about the battle for North Africa and the Mediterranean is that it was the only theatre of war from 1940-1944 where the British Army seriously took on the Wehrmacht. Compared with what happened elsewhere the numbers engaged were very small. Yet strategically the theatre was crucial — indeed so important was it that had we not held on to it, it is difficult to see how the war against Germany could have been successfully waged. I intend to concentrate on the land campaign.

Michael Howard observed that after the fall of France there was for Britain no prospect of a successful decision against Germany. Yet there was a subsidiary theatre where British forces could be employed to harass the enemy and perhaps inflict serious damage, for Italy's entry into the war turned the Middle East into an active area of operations.

This was well understood by Churchill who boldly reinforced the Middle East when the threat of direct invasion of Britain itself was by no means over. Never doubting the grave consequences of losing Egypt and the Middle East, he resolutely declared that the British would fight to the last 'inch and ounce' for Egypt. The desert flank he described as 'the peg on which all else hung'. The CIGS, Sir Alan Brooke, emphatically endorsed this view. He was clear that our strategy must be to conquer North Africa in order to re-open the Mediterranean and attack Italy.

Luckily Hitler did not see things like this. While ready to come to Italy's aid early in 1941 when Mussolini's armies were doing so badly in Cyrenaica and the Balkans, he was not willing, despite eloquent pleadings by Admiral Raeder, to take his eyes off Russia. Raeder urged the Führer to concentrate on war against Britain, particularly in the Mediterranean. Since Italy was weak, he argued, Britain would try to strangle her first, and to make this easier, Britain would aim to get control of north-west Africa. Therefore Germany must prevent it. Assisted by Spain and Vichy France, Gibraltar must be seized and French North Africa secured. Then, with the Italians, German forces should capture the Suez canal and advance through Palestine and Syria to Turkey. "If we reach that point," Raeder concluded, "Turkey will be in our power. The Russian problem will then appear in a different light."

But the Führer had set his heart on Operation *Barbarossa* and once he had embarked on it in June 1941, the die was cast. So that the British were once more able to indulge their predilection for the indirect approach. Indeed unless they elected not to engage Axis forces on land at all, there was no other choice. In any case they had to respond to the advance into Egypt by Graziani's 10th Army in September 1940. No commander, recorded Ciano in his diary, ever undertook a military operation so much against his will. But Mussolini insisted. Thus the stage was set for constant toing and froing in the desert for the next $2^1/_2$ years. The campaign was rather like that of Wellington in the Peninsula. Each was characterised by a dramatic sequence of advances and withdrawals.

Wellington's shuffling to and from Lisbon was mirrored by the Benghazi Stakes with El Alamein as another Torres Vedras. Right up to the end the resemblance persisted. Wellington's last move forward and Montgomery's first one were made possible only because the enemy's main forces were engaged elsewhere by a powerful ally.

Of course this African land campaign could not have been conducted at all without the Royal Navy and the Royal Air Force, who held their own at sea and in the air despite heavy odds against them. The battle for North Africa was above all a battle for supplies, and one of its most renowned players was the tiny fortress of Malta. Sea and air offensives launched from Malta would keep Axis forces in North Africa short of the indispensable sinews of war, and so enable 8th Army to go forward, capture airfields closer to Malta, bring air support to our convoys and so sharpen Malta's sting. To suppress Malta therefore was for the Axis of great moment. German naval and air reinforcements would then swing the pendulum back in their favour; Axis blows at the island would multiply; Malta's inability to strike back would allow the Afrika Korps to receive the supplies it so badly needed, and then at the very time when hanging on to desert airfields became crucial for Malta's survival, the 8th Army would be faced with a resurgent enemy. In short the British had to keep Malta if the 8th Army were to advance, while the 8th Army had to advance if the British were to keep Malta. This was the conundrum.

Closely linked was the matter of L of C. In the desert war, one side or the other was usually closer to its main base; its opponent therefore would be at the end of long L of C. The former was strong in logistics, strong in air support, strong in balance and strong in offensive capability. The latter was likely to be weak in all four. British and Axis forces each had their turn. First — the situation in late 1940.

Wavell's offensive against the Italian 10th Army lasted from December 1940 to February 1941 and was that rare thing — a battle of annihilation. O'Connor, who conceived and commanded it, displayed the sort of driving personal leadership at the front that Rommel was to be famous for later. He was always where he was most needed at critical moments. He went everywhere. He was tireless in maintaining a grip on his small, but elusive force. His watchword was offensive action whenever possible. The Australians, never prodigal with their praise of British commanders, said: "Do you know what we call your general? The little terrier — because he never let's go!"

What O'Connor and his men achieved was remarkable. In two months two British divisions advanced 500 miles and routed an army of ten divisions. They captured 130,000 enemy soldiers, 400 tanks, 800 guns. The Royal Air Force established mastery of the skies and destroyed 150 enemy aircraft. But the RAF's contribution was not to be measured in numbers of aircraft destroyed. They allowed the tanks and armoured cars of O'Connor's tiny force to outflank the enemy without interruption by air attack and to emerge unsuspected behind the enemy columns.

O'Connor wanted to go on to capture Sirte and Tripoli, and Wavell backed him, but was overruled by Churchill, who had decided that Germany's attack on Greece must be countered. Greece had to be 'succoured' as Churchill put it. The CIGS recalled that when he tried to convince the Prime Minister that all the troops in the Middle East were fully committed and that none could be spared for Greece, Churchill turned on him, blood rushing to his great neck, eyes darting fury and began to talk of Courts Martial and firing squads in Cairo. The CIGS regretted not having thought until later of asking Churchill whom he wanted to shoot.

Hitler also decided to support the Italian position in North Africa so that Tripolitania would not be lost. Accordingly he despatched Fliegerkorps X to Sicily to attack British forces in the Mediterranean, in Cyrenaica and in Egypt. What is more, the Deutsches Afrika Korps under command of Lieutenant-General Erwin Rommel was sent to Tripoli. It was soon clear that a new chapter had opened in desert fighting, and that from this time until late 1942, the tune would largely be called by the dashing blitzkrieg tactics of the Desert Fox. One vital feature of these tactics was that the Afrika Korps fought with all-arms teams of tanks, armoured infantry, artillery and anti-tank guns — a devastating combination which the British never seemed to understand or master. And the dreaded 88mm anti-tank gun was never matched in range or effect by a British gun.

Between March and April 1941 Rommel and his panzers, ably supported by Stukas, brought a new set of rules to the desert and bundled the British right out of Cyrenaica back into Egypt, leaving only Tobruk in British hands.

Rommel later gave his views on Hitler's strategic mistakes at this time. Germany, he said, should have kept her hands off Greece and concentrated on North Africa to drive the British right out of the Mediterranean area. Malta should have been taken, not Crete. Capture of the whole British-held coastline would have isolated south-east Europe, and turned the British out of the Middle East. The prize would have been incalculable. Rommel and Raeder thought alike.

In May 1941 Raeder renewed his proposal for a 'decisive Egypt-Suez offensive for that autumn which would be more deadly to the British Empire than the capture of London'. Certainly the moment was opportune. Wavell and his fellow C-in-C were harder pressed and more stretched than at any other time. The East African campaign was not over; Greece and Crete had taken their toll of men and material, including grievous naval losses; Malta must be kept supplied; Tobruk turned into a fortress; Rashid Ali's pro-German rising in Iraq had to be suppressed; Syria to be invaded and occupied; Rommel to be attacked. This last need was especially urgent, as possession of Crete enabled the Axis to open sea communications with Cyrenaica via western Greece. This route must therefore be interfered with. To do so, to help Malta and to go on attacking the Tripoli sea route, airfields in eastern Cyrenaica must be re-captured. Therefore the enemy in the Western Desert must be brought to battle and destroyed.

Easily said! Wavell failed to defeat Rommel and got the sack from Churchill. Auchinleck replaced him, and for the time being the desert flank — 'the peg on which all else hung' — held. Had the Wehrmacht reinforced Rommel with even a tenth of the panzer and air power allotted to *Barbarossa*, the assault on Russia, it is difficult to see how Great Britain could have held the Middle East base. And, as the *Official History* put it: "Had the Eastern Mediterranean area not been successfully held during the lean years, in which case for want of bases, no British fleet or air forces could have even disputed the control of the Mediterranean sea communications, the task of the Allies in gaining a foothold in Europe would have been rendered immensely more difficult; indeed it might well have proved to be beyond their powers". Fortunately for the Allies, in June 1941 Germany had turned away from the Mediterranean.

Having replaced Wavell with Auchinleck in the hope that the latter would soon attack Rommel, Churchill had to wait until November 1941 before he did. The *Crusader* battle may be likened to Napoleon's attack on the Prussians at Ligny, two days before Waterloo. It mauled the Afrika

Korps, but did not destroy it. It was true that Rommel had been forced back, Tobruk relieved and Cyrenaica retaken. Yet 8th Army had lost 20,000 men and administratively was at the end of its tether. Moreover Rommel was soon to strike again in a way more deadly than ever.

While *Crusader* was in progress two remarkable things happened. First, Japan attacked the United States and the British. Secondly, Hitler committed a colossal strategic blunder by declaring war on the United States. A meeting between British and American leaders then laid down broad plans for prosecuting the war. Japan would be denied the means to wage war, while the Allies concentrated on Germany. They would tighten the ring around Germany — by supporting Russia, by strengthening their Middle East position and by seizing the whole of the North African coast. This last undertaking led to an Allied decision in July 1942 to mount an Anglo-American invasion of north-west Africa. Thus Roosevelt would fulfil his promise to Stalin that the US Army would begin to fight the German Army before the end of that year.

July 1942 also saw the British position in the Middle East at its lowest ebb, for in May Rommel attacked the 8th Army at Gazala, swept all before him, captured Tobruk and advanced right to the El Alamein line. Churchill went to Cairo and appointed the winning team of Alexander and Montgomery. Close to its supply base and substantially reinforced, it was an easy matter for Montgomery's 8th Army to defeat Rommel's final fling at Alam Halfa in September 1942. Montgomery now prepared for his great set piece battle.

At Alamein he not only enjoyed great material superiority, but the Desert Air Force was at the peak of its strength and skill, while *Ultra* — the cipher breaking device which enabled the British to read the German High Command signals — gave Montgomery complete and continuous information about Rommel's supply situation and his intentions.

8th Army had about 200,000 fighting men while Rommel's Panzerarmee had 100,000, half German, half Italian. Tedder had 530 serviceable aeroplanes against 350. Logistically the two sides were totally uneven. 8th Army had everything it needed and more. The Panzerarmee had only enough fuel and ammunition for about ten days normal consumption. The choice before Rommel was thus either to fight the battle and by virtue of numbers and logistics, lose it; or give up the benefits of favourable ground with immensely deep minefields and not fight it at all. In the event it was a hard struggle, despite superb support from the Desert Air Force. After the break-in on 23rd October, came a bitter dog-fight, then defeat of Rommel's counter-attack, a switch of 8th Army's main axis, and finally the break-out from 3rd-7th November. Next day Anglo-American forces landed in north west Africa Operation *Torch*. All that

Rommel could do now was to fight a delaying action, while von Arnim in Tunis held the British, French and American forces at bay — for a time. From November 1942, therefore, there was not one land battle for North Africa, but two. Not for three months would their efforts be concentrated under a single command.

Meanwhile the Allied leaders, Churchill and Roosevelt and their Chiefs of Staff, meet at Casablanca, and it was here that the so-called Mediterranean Strategy was agreed. The problem facing these great men, realising as they did that there would not be enough men or material to mount cross-Channel operations before 1944, was how to make use of North Africa to speed up the defeat of Germany. They agreed that there should be three objectives — to open the Mediterranean and so release shipping; to divert German pressure from Russia; and to force Italy to capitulate.

In February 1943 Rommel took command of Army Group Africa. He struggled to find some way of inflicting defeat on his enemies, but his shortage of supplies made it impossible. After a last spoiling attack on 8th Army at Medenine, Rommel left Africa, never to return. He had been the brightest star in the whole campaign, and would still have much to do in Normandy. Meanwhile 8th Army advanced from the east and 1st Army from the west. At sea and in the air the battle for supply and reinforcement was decisively won by the Allies. At length General Alexander issued orders for an Army Group battle to capture Tunis and Bizerta. Von Arnim's forces were simply overwhelmed, and on 13th May 1943 HQ Afrika Korps sent a signal saying that all ammunition had been shot off, arms and equipment had been destroyed and that it could fight no more. On the same day Alexander sent a message to Churchill declaring that the campaign was over, that the Allies were masters of the North African shores and that he awaited further orders. What, asked Churchill, to whom the redemption of this continent had been so great a goal, were they to do with their victory? He was not slow to answer his own question.

He was determined that the British and Allied armies in the Mediterranean should not stand idle. At Casablanca it had been agreed that Sicily should be invaded to distract German forces and put further pressure on Italy. After that the goal would be Italy itself. Churchill always maintained that a right-handed thrust into southern Europe and a left-handed thrust across the Channel should be complementary, and each could be exploited as opportunity and resources permitted. This strategy of exploiting success in North Africa was clearly sound and correct. The distraction of the Italian campaign *did* cause the Germans to move valuable divisions away from the Russian front and away from where the

20 THE END OF THE BEGINNING

Normandy landings were to take place. The Mediterranean strategy may have been a subsidiary one, but it was still an irreplaceable stepping stone to victory in the West.

May I conclude by saying that through all these campaigns, the courage and devotion to duty of the individual soldiers, sailors and airmen — no matter from which countries they came — shine like beacons, undimmed and never to be forgotten.

Chairman

Our later focus on the detail of these campaigns would mean little without the perspective General Strawson has just given us. Our next speaker is also very well known to anyone with an interest in military history: Mr Humphrey Wynn. He served as an RAF pilot from 1940 to 1946, during which time he flew for nine months (1942/3) on the West African Reinforcement Route. On leaving the regular Air Force he went on to serve with the RAFVR from 1948 to 1980; he had been public relations officer for the SBAC and the Air League and before joining the Air Historical Branch he was also Deputy Editor and Defence Correspondent of the aviation magazine Flight International. He has written a history on the post-war bomber role, a history of the RAF strategic nuclear deterrent, and he was co-author of that very interesting book "Prelude to Overlord".

He will now take up the story in the Mediterranean theatre by telling us what organisational shape the Air Force was in in the Western Desert; he will cover the confused higher command organisation, and in particular he will tell us how the maintenance and support facilities were organised to support the campaign, including the vital question of reinforcement and replacement from the home base, which at that time was a very long way away indeed.

5. The RAF in the Mediterranean Theatre

Mr Humphrey Wynn

When Italy entered the war on 10 June 1940 the RAF had a very small force in the Western Desert — only five squadrons, of Gladiators, Blenheims and Bombays. With the Army, this guarded the Egyptian border. There were about 250 aircraft in Middle East Command as a whole, compared with the Italians' 570 in Libya and Italian East Africa.

Within the next two years, with the intervention of the Afrika Corps and Luftwaffe from February 1941, air and land fighting had swept back and forth through the Cyrenaican and Western Deserts; and despite the uncertain and dangerous value of the Mediterranean as a supply and reinforcement route, the original small RAF presence had grown into an Allied Air Force of over a thousand aircraft in some 60 squadrons capable of every kind of offensive role.

For, uniquely among RAF Commands, the Middle East had created a complete Air Force — Interceptors, ground-attack aircraft, light, medium and heavy bombers, night fighters, reconnaissance, maritime and transport aircraft. How this had been achieved in such a short time despite losses sustained in the back-and-forth desert battles and the disastrous diversions of the Greece and Crete campaigns, is the theme of this contribution to today's proceedings. It resulted largely from two factors: the supply of British and American aircraft shipped to African ports; and the support given to the Desert Air Force by the supply, maintenance and repair organisation, which was radically overhauled and reorganised during 1941.

Before referring to these changes — which brought the Middle East Command from a peacetime to a wartime footing in a few crucial months — the one constant factor in the continually changing pattern of desert warfare should be stressed: an operational environment of sand, dust and stones — inimical to any kind of mechanically propelled vehicle and making life that much more difficult for aircrew and groundcrew — plus heat and flies, common and persistent enemies on both sides of the battlefield; while every advance or retreat meant longer — or more disorganised — lines of supply and communication, with water, food, fuel and ammunition all No 1 priorities.

The key to successful operations by the Desert Air Force in a moving battle, with the close co-operation which had been developed between airmen and soldiers, was re-supply and support. This had to be as mobile as the squadrons themselves, which had to be provided with replacement aircraft, fuel and ammunition, wherever they might be and however fast the advance.

The logistic key to the support of the squadrons existed in the RSUs (Repair and Salvage Units), which supplied their new aircraft, retrieved their crashed ones and took back their battle-worn and damaged ones for rebuilding. The part played by the Hudson transport squadrons in flying up ammunition to forward landing-grounds, or moving the squadrons themselves, should also not be forgotten.

Behind the RSUs were the maintenance Units in the Delta area. Their numbers and activities increased enormously from 1941 onwards as a result of the initiative of the new AOC-in-C, Air Marshal Tedder, as I shall describe. The MUs specialised in aircraft, engines, ammunition, fuel and motor transport and employed thousands of Egyptian civilian workers under the jurisdiction of RAF personnel.

In 1939-41 there were four MUs serving the RAF in the Middle East — Nos 102 (which was bombed in August 1941), 103, 107 and 111, plus the British Airways Repair Unit at Heliopolis and an Auxiliary Repair Depot at Helwan. By 1941-43 there were nine Maintenance Units supporting the Desert Air Force; and the cause of this increase — a radical reorganisation of the Middle East maintenance, repair and supply set-up — will subsequently be made clear.

These MUs received the new aircraft which flowed into the theatre along the African reinforcement routes — mainly from Takoradi on the Gold Coast and from Port Sudan on the Red Sea, harbours with dock facilities into which they were shipped and then assembled and test-flown.

The West African route had been pioneered in pre-war years (one of the earliest RAF flights — from Cairo to northern Nigeria — having been led by 'Mary' Coningham, AOC the Desert Air Force, in the 1930s when he was a Squadron Leader) and it was opened up from September 1940.

The route from Takoradi to Egypt was nearly 3,700 miles long, over inhospitable but largely British-controlled terrain, therefore invulnerable to enemy interference. The penalty was the addition of up to 22 engine/airframe hours before the aircraft got to MUs to be prepared for operational use. By mid-1941 the flow of machines along this route was reaching a total of 180 per month, though this figure fluctuated owing to the irregularity of shipping arrivals at Takoradi. The West African Reinforcement Route, controlled by Air Commodore H K Thorold at its Gold Coast end, was a masterpiece of organisation, engineering and airmanship. Spitfires, Hurricanes, and Kittyhawks flew in convoys of eight led by a Blenheim or a Boston whose crew were responsible for navigation. The longest stage was 690 miles — 3^1/$_2$ hours in a Hurricane. The fighters' cockpit hoods were painted white as protection from the sun — from which there was no escape, flying on a steady course.

While the 1941 battles of the Mediterranean war were being fought, there was an organisational one to be fought and won in Egypt. As Commander-in-Chief, Air Marshal Tedder had manifold responsibilities covering a vast area — from the border with Vichy French territory in the north-east to West Africa, Kenya and Aden in the south. But he knew that his most urgent task was to improve the supply of serviceable aircraft in his Command — a supply which had fallen to a dangerously low level early in 1941 after the reverses in Cyrenaica, Greece and Crete.

The main problem was that the hierarchy of the Middle East Air Force, under which maintenance and supply came under the Air Officer Administration — however hard and long he worked and however conscientious he was, could not cope with the hugely increased demand once the Luftwaffe had entered the fray. MEAF, an Air Force in itself, needed something comparable with Maintenance Command in the UK.

This problem had been recognised in London and Lord Beaverbrook, Minister of Aircraft Production, had suggested to the War Cabinet that Air Vice-Marshal Graham Dawson should be sent out to Cairo. This was agreed to on 9 May 1941 and Tedder, who had known Dawson in the MAP, wanted him to become Chief Maintenance and Supply Officer — directly under himself — and also wanted a Maintenance Group to be established. The original aim of Dawson's mission to the Middle East was to investigate and solve the supply and maintenance problems in the Command.

He was then 46, a senior officer of great experience. He had been seriously wounded when serving in the RNAS at Gallipoli in 1915; he was both a pilot and an engineer, a unique combination of skills which fitted him well for the tasks ahead; and he was a man of strong character who knew exactly what he wanted and was not afraid to tell anyone — particularly someone whose performance he considered inadequate — exactly what he thought.

Ironically, in view of his great contribution to the Middle East air war from 1941 to 1944, his name does not appear in the Air Force List among the MEAF hierarchy for that period — because he was still, in Establishment terms, with the Ministry of Aircraft Production.

Dawson and his four-man team of experts (Air Commodore Boswell, Group Captain Leigh and Wing Commanders Barber and Bernard) left the UK on 16 May and travelled by air to Egypt along one of the main arteries of supply — via Gibraltar, Freetown, Takoradi and the West African Reinforcement Route. On their way they suggested and made changes — some of them painful to the personnel concerned.

In Cairo, Air Vice-Marshall Dawson — who was equal in rank to the Air Officer Administration, under whom the Air Ministry wished him to work — took up the post of Chief Maintenance and Supply Officer; and a new Maintenance Group, No 206, was formed — to control all the MUs, RSUs and ASPs (Air Stores Parks).

These changes perturbed the Air Ministry; but when an Establishment Committee visited Cairo in the autumn of 1941, they found they had nonetheless been put into effect. Such was Tedder's quiet determination: he won the organisational battle which was crucial to success in the desert battles. Eventually, the existence of the CMSO as the third main branch of the AOC-in C's staff was officially recognised.

No 206 Group was commanded by Air Commodore C B Cooke, who had been Chief Maintenance Officer before Dawson's arrival and had worked with him on changes to improve the situation.

Under the new management, additional Repair and Salvage Units were formed — all of them fully mobile. A Base Salvage Depot was established in the Delta area to repair crashed aircraft which the RSUs could not deal with. Workshops were set up wherever space could be found for them — however insalubrious the environment. The Tura Caves south of Cairo — stonemasonry sites for the building of the Pyramids — were opened-up for engine repairs and as equipment stores. The supply side of the CMSO's organisation — getting new aircraft to the Desert Air Force squadrons — was represented by an increasing flow to the Maintenance Units from the trans-African routes, from convoys which struggled bravely through the Mediterranean under Royal Navy protection, or direct from the UK in the shape of bombers flown out under cover of darkness by newly trained crews.

At the time of Dawson's arrival in the Middle East in mid-1941 there were only some 200 aircraft serviceable and available for operations. By the time of the El Alamein offensive in October 1942 there were about 1,500. Commenting on the build-up for that battle, Tedder noted that "only a formation of the additional maintenance units required to support the 60 squadron programme — in advance of Air Ministry permission — has enabled the squadrons to put up their unprecedented effort in recent months". Typically, he added that it was only by "the tireless and superhuman efforts of so-called 'surplus' fitters and riggers that we have been able to come anywhere near meeting the wastage in the Western Desert". What he meant is illustrated by the figures: out of 858 aircraft issued to units between 8 September and 23 October 1942, only 480 were new arrivals: the remaining 378 had been repaired in Egypt — an indication of the great effort made by the maintenance and repair organisation.

It is sad to record that Graham Dawson, who by improving and energising it made such an immense contribution to victory in the desert air war and the advance from El Alamein, lost his life in a flying accident in November 1944 — when en route by Liberator from Algiers to Brussels to meet his old chief and friend Sir Arthur Tedder, who in 1941 had seen what needed to be done and had found in Dawson the ideal man for the job.

Chairman

As a former AMSO on the Air Force Board I found myself applauding very warmly the emphasis Humphrey has put on this very important aspect of the campaign, without which we should very quickly have lost it.

We now turn to Air Chief Marshal Sir Freddy Rosier.

6. How the Joint System Worked (1)

Air Chief Marshal Sir Frederick Rosier

Maybe Sir Kenneth Cross should have spoken first — but knowing Group Captain Cross I insisted I should be put first and he would then correct my mistakes.

At dawn one morning in early June 1941 after a welcome break in Gibraltar while the Navy went off to chase the Bismarck, my squadron flew off the carrier HMS Furious for Malta and then on to Egypt. There we found the RAF were much in disfavour, being blamed for lack of support in Greece and Crete — much the same as it had been after Dunkirk. When I got to the Desert later that month operation Battleaxe had ended in stalemate and there was little activity by the ground forces. However, the fighter force which was based some hundred miles back from the forward landing grounds at Sidi Barrani was kept reasonably busy on such tasks as the occasional Tac R escort defensive patrols over the forward areas, local air defence particularly of Mersa Matruh, escorting slow moving ships going to Tobruk. That latter task was very bad for the nerves, particularly in the late afternoons when the ships were only a few miles away from the German landing grounds at Gambut and every so often there were Stukas escorted by Me 110s and 109s arriving without any warning out of the setting sun.

We came under the control of a fighter wing but my clearest memory is of the impact of the Group AOC; he was a famous World War I Ace, Air Cdre Collishaw, Canadian. He used to come up with all kinds of ideas which he would preface by slapping his knee and saying "got a clue, see". Then to our relief we were able to talk him out of most of these, for while they might have been good against the Italians the Germans were a different lot. In September I was attached to AHQ Western Desert which had replaced the Group and was under the command of 'Mary' Coningham, an impressive figure. Whilst there, incidentally, the Wing Commander Training and I prevailed on him to let us go up to the forward area where there were stories of some Italian Stukas which had force-landed out of fuel. We managed to get to one of them and semi-successfully flew it back.

This attachment was short-lived; in early October I took over a newly formed fighter wing, the other coming under the then Group Captain Cross. The wings were so organised that each could control the whole fighter force numbering some 13 squadrons including a Navy squadron with a mixed bag of fighters. We were self-contained, fully mobile, and the concept was that during advances or retreats the two wings by leap-frogging would maintain continuous control of operations. In many respects the wings were similar to the 83 and 84 Group Control Centres later in the war. The relationship between the wings, and between them and AHQ, were very close, with the AOC prepared to allow us much discretion in making operational decisions. In that same month the system whereby the air could give direct support to the ground forces was agreed, and steps were taken to provide the communications, and this was followed by an Ops Instruction which contained the all-important statement that air support bombing demanded a large degree of air superiority, the gaining of which was the first task of the Air Forces. Time would show that air superiority would produce a greater range of advantages than this, but it was a good first step.

Just before and during the next offensive — Crusader — the fighter force having moved to forward landing grounds, mostly south of Sidi Barrani at a place called St Maddalena, the force was engaged in fighter sweeps, escort to bombers, Tac R and offensives against airfields, aircraft and MT and supply concentrations. There was also the Tobruk shipping commitment. At the time our fighters — Hurricanes and Tomahawks mostly — were inferior in performance to the 109s, while the German AA defences were far more effective. Nevertheless despite high casualties we kept on with efforts to gain a favourable air situation and when we took over the landing grounds vacated by the enemy it was heartening to see the number of aircraft destroyed and damaged which had been left on them. Incidentally just after the start of Crusader a lot of 109s stopped me getting to Tobruk, where I was going to set up an advance base, and a few days later after a lot of walking I was welcomed back by Group Captain Cross!

There is no doubt that, had the Army been able to give us realistic bomb lines, had there been some means of differentiating between enemy and friendly ground forces in the battle area, and had their calls for support reached us more quickly, we could have provided much more close air support than we did. Army commanders themselves often knew less about the position of their own forces than we did, and confusion prevailed for much of the time.

In the next two months we leap-frogged all the way to Antelat and we leapfrogged back again to El Adem and Gambut. Early one morning as the Group Captain and I were shaving — and I think there was an enemy force not far away — he turned to me and said "You know, Fred, a shave every morning makes all the difference between an orderly withdrawal and a disorderly rout". With the retreat being checked on the Gazala Line, we had a good set-up for both offensive and defensive operations, helped greatly by a forward radar at Gazala and by a 'Y' unit, which provided us with a lot of tactical intelligence — they were excellent. However, our operational effectiveness then was not good; replacements for our heavy losses were a problem; several of the squadrons had been withdrawn for re-equipment. Furthermore our aeroplanes were proving less and less effective. We badly needed Spitfires to counter the 109s, and Kittyhawks for general use. Very slowly we began to get them.

During that time too there were organisational changes. Our two Wings were merged into a Fighter Group, No 211, and the fighter squadrons which had previously been administered directly by AHQ were banded together by aircraft types into new type wings. While we were there, there were rumours that the other side had women. This prompted an ALO of mine to produce a piece of paper which he brought to me. It was headed "The Flying Brothel" and went something like this:

"Gestapo spies amongst our forces investigate subversive sources in which Teutons sensing spring agitate to have their fling, and Wilhelmstrasse too finds of late a tendency towards spring. So a meeting was called — Herr Kuts suggested reading Freud, at which Hitler got a bit annoyed; then Goering more than filled the breach by saying Gentlemen I have means in reach to solve this burning problem for you — flying brothel is the thing to solve the urgency of spring. So Berlin was scoured and Dresden too, to find sufficient trollops who enjoyed the joys of copulation but were still au fait with aviation. And now the scheme has reached fruition — our troops are in first class condition, for though the ersatz food may cloy, they still can get their strength through joy".

This is the first time an audience has heard it.

When Rommel started his next attack at the end of May, air operations in direct support of our ground forces were again hindered by the same sort of confusion as had prevailed in Crusader, while our ability to intercept his raids — particularly those against Bir Hakeim — was affected when our forward radar had to be withdrawn from Gazala. With the fall of Bir Hakeim and Tobruk, Rommel continued his advance towards Egypt, though he was getting little support from his air forces. Fortunately we were able during that retreat to maintain almost continuous attacks against the enemy columns while keeping our own ground forces free from enemy air interference. Thank God we were able to do it, because they were toe to tail. In his book "The North African Campaign", Sir William

Jackson writes "It was the RAF that was the real British fighting force at the time". Its morale was very high as it rose to the occasion of saving the 8th Army. I should make it clear that we also had Australian and South African squadrons.

I suppose it was during the Battle of Alam Halfa, which started with another Rommel attack, that air support was seen at its best. Except when sandstorms interfered, the enemy ground forces were attacked by day and night. Writing of this battle, Liddell Hart says: "Most important of all was the well gauged combination of air power with the ground forces plan, The Air Forces could operate the more freely and effectively because of being able to count on all troops within the ring as being enemy, in contrast to the way in which air action is handicapped in a more fluid kind of battle". The Rommel Papers too are illuminating on this. That operation showed what could be achieved by Army and Air commanders talking to each other and by the joint planning of air and ground action. This was the time when Montgomery and Coningham saw eye to eye on the means of getting the best dividends out of their action. I remember a briefing by Montgomery where he said "I have brought you together to tell you that I have made a plan — and when I say I've made a plan it's not quite right because I've made a plan in conjunction with the Air Force. Every plan has to have an intention — mine is to go to Tripoli, and it's the intention of the Air Force too to go to Tripoli. In fact we 're all going to Tripoli together". Quite remarkable — at the end we had no doubt we were going to Tripoli!

After Alamein a long, laborious, rather tedious advance took place. Alamein had proved a tough battle, air support of all kinds contributing much to the victory. By then our fighter force was in much better shape, with more Spitfires and Kittyhawks, and the addition of a Group of the USAAF. Also more and more fighters had been converted to carry bombs. The experiment of using a Hurricane with a pair of 40mm cannon had not been much of a success.

In my 20 months in the Desert being leaving from Tripoli, certain points had become clear. Although costly, the fight for and maintenance of air superiority had been of fundamental importance. It had given both the Army and Air Force freedom of action. Lack of accurate, timely information on the mission of our ground force units had often resulted in the Army being ultra cautious, stipulating bomb lines so far away from its units that the Air Force was prevented from operating in close support. The time lag between the initiation of Army requests for close support and their receipt by the Air Force, together with the longer time taken by light bombers to get to the target areas, had resulted in the fighter bombers becoming increasingly important. Most of the ground targets attacked from the air came from Tac R and from armed recce sorties by fighters, not from the Army. Tac Rs often had to be supported either by fighter escort or by diversionary flights. Tasking of Tac R by an Army unit in isolation resulted in undue losses. Lastly, sound operational planning demanded a joint approach by Army and Air Force.

Chairman

The Air Marshal has reminded us of the ubiquity of air power and given us humour and even poetry as well. Our next speaker, Sir Kenneth Cross, joined the RAF in 1930, became a fighter pilot, and in 1939/40 was a squadron commander in this country, in France and in Norway. In North Africa he was OC of an air defence wing in Egypt, headed a fighter wing in the Western Desert, AOC the air defence group, Benghazi, then AOC 242 Group with the First Army in Tunisia and later in Sicily. He held a number of very senior posts thereafter, including AOC of a Group in Bomber Command, C in C Bomber Command and C in C Transport Command. He retired in 1968. He will pick up the story of the reorganisation of the Air Forces, with the command arrangements in the theatre. He will tell us of the doctrine and the systems for air/land co-operation, the various roles of air power that evolved, and some of the lessons that emerged.

6. How the Joint System Worked (2)

Air Chief Marshal Sir Kenneth Cross, KCB, CBE, DSO, DFC

You will see what I had to put up with in the Desert! There was nothing Fred said that I would disagree with, except that on the occasion when he was shot down by a 109 we had discussed for some time the use of a radar set which had been left behind in Tobruk and could read over the enemy airfields. We weren't getting much good information out of this station, and we needed to send there someone who knew what we wanted. We looked at each other and I was senior to Fred, so he had to go. We gave him an escort of three Kittyhawk squadrons, and within the hour they returned in bits and pieces. I went straight over to the dispersal and asked about the Wing Commander. "Yes he was on the tail of a 109 and going well". "But did he get into Tobruk?" I asked. "I don't know about that — but he was going well". So Fred was missing. Then, unable to get to Tobruk he was on his way back, saw a Kittyhawk belly land and the pilot get out, went down to pick him up and burst a tyre. He then walked back, taking two days; his replacement having arrived from Cairo, Fred came in, having survived again.

I joined the Desert Air Force at Crusader. The RAF and Army had no doctrine on how to operate together. All Generals want two things: they need to know what is on the other side of the hill, and they want fire power to remove a block when they are advancing. When starting Crusader, we had ample reconnaissance and we had 140 bombers to provide the fire power. As for air superiority, the Army commanders were highly suspicious of the term; it seemed to mean the Air Force enjoying themselves instead of looking after them. We had 350 fighters, Tedder having stripped the Delta of fighters in order to send them all forward to the Desert; there had been questions from the New Zealand government after the experiences of Greece and Crete. So we had a sizeable force, but all inferior to the 109. In Crusader, however, we overwhelmed them in numbers and achieved a high degree of air superiority over the battlefield. General Freyburg, who had been a major questioner in these matters, sent a message: "I think your fellows are simply magnificent and all my men are saying the same thing".

At this time the Air Support Signals made its appearance; this was supposed to be the means by which the Army could request attacks on targets by the bomber force. The bombers were at a high state of readiness but sat there and were never used. Meanwhile the fighter wings were asking why we were not bombing these targets — all tightly bunched and marvellous targets. At one point Rommel swept round the rear of our attacking forces; we reported it in mid-morning but it was only identified as an attacking column in mid-afternoon. What emerged was the certainty that the air would know what was going on, because they would see it and report it all the time — from the ground one could not see more than two miles. Fred and I discussed this all the time; we knew what we could do to help them, whereas they did not. It was a real muddle, something which we airmen were not used to. It took a long time to sink in that we were equal partners, and that it was better for us to tell the Army what we could do to help them than for them to tell us.

I left the Desert after the Casablanca Conference when Tedder went over to the other side and I was sent to command the Group that was supporting the First Army. It was a splendid army, but had been in England for a long time with no fighting. Their discipline was tremendous, but they knew nothing about war so we went through again all the problems we had had with the 8th Army.

For example when I went to see General Anderson (I was aged 30; he was much older), he said he wanted me to quarter the ground in front of his advancing infantry. I said I had no experience of that sort of thing and in any case got my directives from North African Tactical Air Forces under Coningham. Letting that one go he then said he could not send a despatch rider anywhere without his being knocked off his bicycle by a 190; what could I do? I replied by suggesting I ask General Doolittle to bomb Tunis docks. What has that to do with my despatch rider, he said. Unfortunately our medium bombers could not operate effectively against such a heavily defended target, and while Doolittle's heavies could clearly do so from greater height he told me they were already fully committed by Washington against targets in Sicily and Southern Italy in preparation for the next round. But Doolittle then went on to say that sometimes the weather was bad, and if we could provide a Spitfire escort he would "do" Tunis. Two days later he did it and all our despatch riders could carry on with their job — because all the 190s were now waiting for him to do it again.

Subsequently, with the approach of the 8th Army from the South, we had overwhelming force on the ground — and in the air, where the biggest danger in the air was from collision. The main lesson was that, once the Army decided what they wanted to do, we were the people to tell them what we could do to help — not the other way round.

Chairman

These valuable lessons are now firmly implanted in our minds for the afternoon. Our last two speakers have given us the flavour of the operational leadership available to the RAF during this campaign and it was particularly interesting to hear from two participants who commanded Wings — junior enough to participate in the air fighting but senior enough to help direct events. Our next speaker is Dr Vincent Orange, a most distinguished historian and one who served for three years in the RAF. He has spent many years in New Zealand where he has lectured on history at the University of Canterbury, where he was elected Associate Member of the New Zealand Aeronautical Society. Most of us are familiar with his biographies of Park and Coningham, both prominent figures in the events we are talking about today. He will discuss something absolutely crucial in military as in other branches of history, yet all too often submerged in the account of events, namely the personalities involved.

7. The Commanders and the Command System

Vincent Orange

In February 1940, Rommel asked a veteran general of the Great War for advice on the best way to command a panzer division. 'You'll find there are always two possible decisions open to you', he was told. 'Take the bolder one — it's always best." Luckily for us, Rommel — backed by Hitler — followed this advice and thereby lost the Axis Powers a royal chance of victory in the Mediterranean War. So my first suggestion to any budding, blossomed or even wilting commanders here present is: 'Get rid of advisers who like epigrams.'

Tedder, a staff college graduate and, worse still, a former staff college *teacher* (the very model of an officer-type loathed by Rommel) would have commented: 'There's a lot of truth in that epigram. However, you should ask yourself not only where you'll be if the bold decision works, but also where you'll be if it doesn't.' In Rommel's case, one answer to the second question was: in front of powerful defences at El Alamein, facing an army with secure supply lines pouring in more of everything every day, whilst his own were very long and suffering constant attack by air and sea. In other words, commanders should temper boldness with forethought and pay attention to logistics. Tedder, Coningham and Park (the three with whom I am chiefly concerned) did; with regard to the Western Desert, Malta and Tunisia (the three areas in which they acted) Rommel and Hitler didn't.

Logistics, as Air Marshal Sir Kenneth Hayr has written, is 'the science of planning and carrying out the movement and maintenance of forces.' Coningham had little grasp of that science — how could he, he never went to staff college — but he recognised its vital importance and Tedder would provide him with an expert assistant in Elmhirst. Rommel had far less grasp than Coningham and, better still, neither a Tedder above him nor an Elmhirst at his side to see that he gave it priority attention. 'Without logistics', wrote Hayr, 'a force has no military utility. Of course a force needs eyes, ears, and teeth, but logistics represents the heart, lungs and lifeblood: it is the life-support system without which the whole force would grind to a halt.' Although Hayr was writing about the recent Gulf War, his words apply equally to all wars. 'Tactics', he concluded (and the Mediterranean War demonstrated) are 'the art of the logistically possible.'

Coningham and Elmhirst, linking operations and logistics out in the Desert, were supported back in Cairo by an excellent team headed by Drummond, Dawson, Pirie and Wigglesworth to manage personnel, technical, repair and maintenance problems, the whole organisation presided over by Tedder. No man, least of all a commander in wartime, is an island, able to function alone; he needs and Tedder, Coningham and Park received — plenty of help. Elmhirst arrived at Coningham's Headquarters in February 1942 and, as Sir Kenneth Cross later recalled, 'he quickly created order where there had been disorder, supply where there had been shortage'. It was Elmhirst who re-organised the Western Desert Air Force into mobile fighter, bomber and reconnaissance wings, all with their own transport. Happily, a friendship grew between Coningham and Elmhirst, to the great advantage of both, for neither could have done the other's job. Another friendship developed with George Beamish, Coningham's choice as Senior Air Staff Officer. The choice is illuminating in three ways: Beamish was a rugby forward of international class who played in a British XV that actually won a Test match in New Zealand; he had won the Sword of Honour at Cranwell (where Coningham himself had served very happily); and he was totally unflappable. Having escaped from the Crete fiasco, nothing that happened in North Africa struck Beamish as really serious. This quality appealed deeply to Coningham who, as Elmhirst once remarked, 'is at his best on days of gloom.'

Individuals on the Axis side may well have matched or surpassed any of these men in ability, but they were not welded into a stable team. Nor were their relations with Berlin and Rome as generally sensible as those of the British commanders with either the Air Ministry or Whitehall. While it may not always have seemed so at the time, it would in retrospect and comparison. Whatever problems these RAF officers had with their masters (service or civilian), their colleagues in other services and later with their American allies, they were nothing like as taxing or as insoluble as those which German and Italian airmen faced when dealing with Rommel in North Africa or Axis authorities in Berlin and Rome.

As one example among many, the Luftwaffe commander (General Hoffman von Waldau) found it even more difficult than did Coningham to get accurate, detailed information on a regular basis from Army commanders about the position of friendly ground forces. Axis forces therefore received far less support than Waldau had available; they were more often bombed in error than British forces and attempts to co-ordinate ground and air attacks were perfunctory. Rommel would begin his fatal invasion of Egypt during the last week of June 1942 without even informing Waldau, let alone waiting for him to move his airfields forward. This decision prevented the Luftwaffe from harassing the British retreat, exposed his own forces to constant aerial attack and denied him the opportunity to inflict serious casualties and generate the panic upon which the success of his invasion depended. In RAF uniform, Waldau might well have compared favourably with Tedder, Coningham and Park; there can be no doubt that he would have relished the steady, powerful support they received in North Africa and Europe.

Nevertheless, my three commanders, by accepting the opportunities they were given and exploiting them brilliantly, deserve great credit. And yet their careers during the Twenties and Thirties were apparently haphazard and chance — rather than planning — assembled them in the Mediterranean. Tedder, for example, had last served there in 1918 and his record up to 1940 suggested a 'nuts and bolts man' (in Churchill's words) who lacked the charisma thought necessary for wartime command. He was, after all, a university graduate who had published a book. These were uncommon feats among senior officers and one not widely regarded as of exceptional value. Worse still, recorded Sir Christopher Foxley Norris, Tedder was 'the sort of chap who always wore his hat slap on the middle of his head.' He had not been a famous fighter pilot in the Great War; he made no dramatic or pioneering flights thereafter; and no boisterous, endearing anecdotes were told of him. 'I wanted to be liked', Tedder said once, 'but I wasn't much.' Even his appointment to Cairo was as second choice to Boyd, whose navigator inadvertently landed him in Sicily. Almost a year later, Tedder's position was still so insecure that one word of criticism to Churchill from Freeman or from Auchinleck would have seen him out of Cairo and back in England, even though he was more nearly a friend of Portal's than any other airman, Freeman excepted. In retrospect, of course, although Tedder's greatness is easy enough to describe as a logical — even inevitable — consequence of his character and experience, he might now be quite unknown but for Boyd's mishap

That same mishap was also Coningham's opportunity when Tedder decided to get rid of Collishaw. He was, thought Tedder, 'a bull in a china shop': too eager to attempt every task in daily operations himself (thereby making his staff officers feel 'frustrated and miserable') and too often foolishly optimistic about what could be done with the available resources in men and aircraft. Tedder could reasonably suppose that Coningham would avoid these faults, but so too might several other officers better known to him. A compelling reason for Coningham's selection was perhaps provided by Ludlow-Hewitt — a wise and grim man, not given to praising lightly or highly. When head of Bomber Command, he had commended Coningham to Portal with unusual warmth and if Portal told this to Tedder, he would have been favourably impressed. On the other hand, Coningham had not served in Egypt for fifteen years; he had had nothing to do with fighters since the end of the Great War; and (uniquely among RAF commanders of the Second World War) he never attended the staff college. Clearly, no-one can hope to command air forces successfully without a college background and though Coningham did his best, his subsequent achievements must stand to Tedder's credit.

Personally, Coningham was everything Tedder was not: famous and much-decorated for his feats as a combat, air display and long-distance pilot; famous also, within the service, for his place in society yachting circles and his prowess at polo and other sports; a man of style, of presence, distinctly non-academic. 'Big, masculine, confident', as Arthur Stanley Gould Lee recalled him 'he had an easy, attractive personality, a ready and colourful flow of talk.' However, Tedder soon learned — if he did not already know — that Coningham's flamboyance masked a strong, self-regarding personality. His 'outstanding characteristic', wrote Sir Philip Joubert, 'lay in his ability to keep his own counsel. I never felt I really knew what was going on behind his dark brown eyes.' Coningham, in other words, was a good *listener*: taking in what was said, not merely waiting a chance to start talking himself (as academics do), and readily using what he heard to shape his own ideas. Except for the sporting and social distinctions, the points made above apply with equal force to Park.

Tedder's job in the Mediterranean was to command *in chief*. That is, to consider strategic options in consultation with his opposite numbers in the Navy and the Army; to deal with the Air Ministry in general and keep open his personal line to Portal in particular; and to oversee the performance of both his Cairo staff and Coningham's air force. He eagerly seized every good reason (and some shaky excuses) to escape into the Desert to see for himself what was going on and to enjoy the exhilaration of being at 'the sharp end'. While there, he practiced one of the more difficult arts of command. Discussing matters with Coningham, he would encourage, congratulate, advise, perhaps even criticise — but he would try not to interfere. It was Coningham's job to command *in the field* and he was entitled to wholehearted support unless or until Tedder felt that serious mistakes were being made, when prompt dismissal should follow.

In fact, Tedder came to regard Coningham — in Liddell Hart's words — as 'the real hero' of the Desert War. The achievements of either Coningham in the Desert or Park in Malta were beyond Tedder. 'He lacked Coningham's easy assurance', wrote Lee, 'and was too highly strung to be able to work continually under the strenuous conditions in which Coningham flourished. But at Cairo, where he sat in the centre and held all the reins, he was able to fulfil his role of higher commander with the greatest skill, organising and disposing his forces, building for the future and devising machinery to work smoothly with the Navy and Army and help link the three Services together for a single purpose.'

Tedder and Coningham liked and respected each other, helped by having different personal qualities yet similar opinions about proper methods of command. With Tedder's approval, Coningham made it his personal business to appoint subordinate commanders, promising them the same absence of interference, the same positive support and the same threat of speedy removal in the event of failure that hovered over his own position. It would not be until August 1942 that these methods would take firm hold in the Eighth Army. Churchill then asked Tedder — a mere airman — what should be done about the chaotic leadership of that army, where orders to senior officers were regarded, by giver and receiver alike, as no more than a useful basis for discussion. Tedder replied that the selection, promotion and removal of commanders should in future be made on the basis of *performance* instead of seniority, friendship, regimental or family connections. The advent of Montgomery would ensure that Tedder's advice was taken.

Tedder and Coningham had the advantage of being second generation commanders in North Africa, while Park represented a third generation in Malta. Their predecessors had had even weaker hands to play and their achievements against the Axis Powers were more than offset by disasters — for which they were not responsible — in Greece, Crete and at sea. To their credit, however, the predecessors of my commanders did at least *identify* problems of combining the punch of fighter and bomber forces with each other and with the efforts of ground forces, together with such vital incidentals as establishing secure, reliable communications, fixing realistic bomblines, ranking targets in order of priority and supplying forward airfields. In addition, all three commanders benefited immensely from steadily-improving lines of supply and intelligence: not only Ultra information about enemy strategy, but Y-service interception of messages in other codes which often yielded information of greater tactical value.

My commanders were also more realistic and more temperate in their dealings with higher authority than their predecessors. Short of modern aircraft, experienced crews and much else, they steered a sensible course between passive acceptance of Air Ministry decisions on the one hand and angry objection to them on the other. They recognised that in fact their needs were as well understood in London as in Cairo and simply could not be adequately met. They therefore gave thanks for what they did receive, improvised with it intelligently, expressed optimism whenever possible and — this above all — *avoided moaning*. Park, following the example of Tedder and Coningham, judged carefully the tone of his signals home. He paid heed to a warning from Bottomley (DCAS) about the number of 'somewhat violent and hasty signals' dispatched by his predecessor. These, wrote Bottomley, had 'tended to fray the nerves and jar the susceptibilities' of people in the Air Ministry who were doing their best to help, who had many worries on their minds — and long memories for bellyachers.

Fortunately, Tedder and Coningham never faced overwhelming enemy strength (as other commanders did in Poland, Scandinavia, France and Russia), though either Park or his predecessor in Malta should have. The Desert was very large, the rival forces very small, the difficulties of supply very great and consequently there were precious intervals between campaigns for reflection and training. But information about tactics evolved in Britain took too long to reach the Desert. As late as October 1941, most pilots were still (as Tedder put it) at a 'village cricket' level of performance. During the following year, however, a 'test match' level of Army-Air co-operation was reached. Increasingly effective use of fighters was made in both combat and escort duties, methods of training, communication, supply, repair and maintenance improved. By November 1942, much was known that could have helped the men employed in Operation Torch. These failures in the transmission of information between Britain and the Desert and later from the Desert back to Britain and on to the United States are typical of an ancient theme in military history: the reluctance of tribes, nations and armed forces to learn except from their own experience. The cost in lives and materials has been so heavy and the instances of defeat suffered or victory delayed so numerous that more serious attention is nowadays paid — not only in staff colleges — to 'lessons learned' than used to be the case.

Tedder had told Coningham to 'get together' with the Army Commander as his *first* task on going out to the Desert. This was, as Coningham wrote after the war, a decision of 'fundamental importance and had a direct bearing on the combined fighting of the two services until the end of the war.' This opinion is supported by that of a Field Marshal, no less (Lord Carver), who has written — when considering air power in the Second World War — that 'by far the most significant contribution (to victory) was made by the tactical air forces in support of the army.' Co-operation, however, whether between or within services is not to be achieved any more easily than a successful marriage. It requires time, goodwill and constant attention far more than rules and regulations. Essential though these are, most systems can be made to work, if goodwill is present. Likewise, all systems can be thwarted if it isn't. Much depends, and always will, upon the personalities of those concerned.

After the fall of Tobruk in June 1942, tedder wrote: 'if only our friend Rommel would run true to form and come bullocking on regardless, there might be a chance of knocking him right out', which is what he did and was was done. Rommel had not grasped, even at that late date, the need to protect his sea supply lines from Malta's attacks. Nor had he grasped the damage done to his land supply lines by Coningham's attacks. Even before the capture of Tobruk, Rommel had wasted nine days in June, using his air force to pound Bir Hacheim, a fortified position held by French troops at the southern end of the Gazala Line. Those days so sapped the Luftwaffe's strength that it proved unable to exploit the British retreat from Gazala to Tobruk, a distance of 35 miles. Coningham's men did well at that time, but should have been tested more severely.

At the end of June, between Gibraltar and the untried, incomplete defences at El Alamein — a distance of over 2,000 miles — Malta was the sole British base. This 'unsinkable aircraft carrier' was anchored a mere 60 miles south of Axis airfields in Sicily. Hitler's decision on 23 June not to attempt its conquest (Operation Hercules) was one of them so fateful of the war. Despite their undoubted skill and determination, Britain's Army, Navy and Air commanders in the Mediterranean could hardly have prevented a conquest of Malta had it been attempted before August 1942 with all the Axis power available. 'I ought to have known', lamented Kesselring after the war, 'that a tactical success can only be exploited and sustained if the supply services are functioning faultlessly.' He ought indeed and so ought the entire Axis war management machine, for it is a point that has decided wars since ancient times.

Park arrived in Malta on 14 July 1942. The task of Malta's RAF Commanders was a classic illustration of air power principles. They had independent control of a fighter battle over the home base, a battle to be followed — once air superiority had been achieved, but only for as long as it could be maintained — by the employment of fighters to escort friendly convoys approaching the island and also to escort bombing raids against targets chosen in consultation with Army and Navy commanders.

Military students have known since Antiquity that it is rarely wise to command defending forces at the outbreak of war because a combination of ill-trained men, inadequate weapons, insufficient supplies and the aggressor's careful preparation will bring defeat and dismissal. But if the defending stage manages to avoid conquest, there may come a time when a combination of well-trained men, adequate weapons, sufficient supplies and the aggressor's mistakes will bring victory and rewards. Although the latter commander may be no more able than the former, he will certainly be better remembered, as both Park in Malta and Montgomery in North Africa would find. It may not be fair, but it is what happens.

Moreover, Park would win a victory in October 1942 that was not in itself difficult. It tested him less severely than several earlier crises in his career, but it was perfectly *timed*. Kesselring had begun his last attack on Malta on 11 October and achieved the worst result. On the one hand, he gave up after only a few days, leaving Park free to carry on attacking Rommel's supply lines. On the other, Kesselring's deployment of half the Luftwaffe's strength to Sicily in order to carry out that attack deprived Rommel of help he would badly need in North Africa before and during the battle of El Alamein. From all Allied points of view, the rest of the war news was bad at the time of Park's victory and he therefore enjoyed a degree of attention from the public prints more appropriate to a pop singer or a tennis player; an attention shortly to be eclipsed, of course, by the blinding light of Montgomery.

Like Coningham, Park was a master of his profession, a good listener, willing to use the ideas of others, a confident battlefield leader and a good co-operator. He thrived on the wide measure of personal influence he had over a major campaign in which air forces played a vital role. He was equally conscious of his image, fashioning a jaunty public manner and eagerly explaining to pilots, ground crews and — not least — the numerous soldiers employed as labourers on his airfields both what was going on and the immense value of their efforts. Park had been the very apostle of defence during the Battle of Britain, but in Malta he recognised the need for offence whenever possible. Commanders are always faced with competing priorities. In this case, unless Malta's aircraft impeded Rommel's build-up, the 8th Army might be defeated again and the fall of Malta would follow that of Egypt no matter how prudently its fuel, ammunition and food stocks had been conserved. Given Ultra and Y-Service intelligence, operations could be planned with the Navy to achieve economy of effort and effect.

Major General Ronald Scobie (GOC Troops in Malta) wrote to Lieutenant General Sir Archibald Nye (Vice-CIGS) at the War Office on 27 September 1942. 'The RAF here are grand', he wrote, 'with a fine commander in Park. They have their opposite number in Sicily completely down at the moment . . . Relations between the services are very good and co-operation is excellent.' Nye replied on 3 December. It has been 'simply thrilling', he wrote, to read of Malta's successes against shipping. These had contributed greatly to Rommel's defeat. 'If you read the English newspapers', he added, 'you get the impression that Rommel was beaten solely by the brilliance of our generals. That, of course, is very good publicity, but it is very bad history!'

The Tunisian Campaign posed fresh challenges to Tedder and Coningham. A different terrain, full of forests and hills; much larger forces employed on either side; the war's first Supreme Commander — an American, reflecting a massive, ever-growing American presence in men as well as material and adding Washington to London as a centre of opinion for Tedder to consider; numerous civilian non-combatants, many of them French subjects; and, not least, a marked contrast between the battle-hardened veterans of the Desert and the inexperienced soldiers and airmen landed in the west. This campaign set a seal of approval upon the methods of Tedder and Coningham, confirming their reputations and so ensuring that they would enjoy high command for the rest of the war.

Coningham greatly impressed Brigadier General Howard A. Craig, USAAF, who recorded his startling opinion that Army and Air Commanders should be equal in status and his even more startling statement that direct support from the air had played only a minor part in Desert conflict. In fact, claimed Coningham (with an exaggeration no doubt calculated to impress Craig still further), the Army had actually been in support of the Air (capturing essential landing grounds, preparing new ones, transporting and protecting supplies) because 'the Army cannot advance without fighters and the fighters cannot move without petrol.'

Until Coningham arrived in Tunisia, another American General (Laurence S. Kuter) was put in charge of something called 'Allied Air Support Command.' 'Since all ground officers are expert Air Chief Marshals', he wrote on 26 January 1943, 'my job is to keep ground forces from swallowing the air forces, to keep RAF from swallowing AAF, etc. Nice bunch of cannibals in Africa! And Casablanca. And London. And Washington.' Coningham, of course, refused to be an 'air support commander' and Kuter foresaw that Spaatz (appointed by Einsenhower as overall air commander) would have a tough time 'between the charming Tedder and the Bellicose Coningham.'

As Spaatz wrote to the Chief of Air Staff in Washington on 8 February, it was hard to treat aviation as 'co-equal with the Army and Navy in our (American) set-up, whereas the RAF will not submit to it being considered in any other way.' It will not accept that air support 'belongs' to an Army Commander or that he may dictate its employment. Spaatz was right and at the end of that same month of February, Portal would emphasise the point again in a letter to Churchill, telling him that the failures in Tunisia before the Desert commanders' arrived had been exacerbated by British and American generals insisting that air power belonged to them and that it should be divided into what he called 'penny packets': that is, numerous small formations of aircraft circling over frontline troops as defensive umbrellas against dive-bomber attacks in particular. Kuter would later recall that Patten refused to camouflage his Command Post and when it was strafed demanded an umbrella from dawn to dusk even if this meant that *no* offensive operations could be flown. According to Kuter, American troops were instructed to abandon light AA weapons and take cover if Stukas appeared, for they were regarded as invincible by men who had seen too many newsreels.

Coningham's address to senior American and british officers (soldiers and Airmen) at Tripoli on 16 February 1943 made a remarkable stir, to judge by the number of copies surviving. This address and a subsequent directive to subordinate commanders summarised principles of lasting value formulated (or remembered) by Tedder, Coningham and those close to them. They were incorporated into a pamphlet, approved by the Air Ministry, by Arnold (head of the USAAF) and by Montgomery who had them widely circulated as his own views throughout the British Army.

These principles may be considered under four headings. Firstly, that the Army and Air Commander must act together in accordance with a combined plan, the whole operation to be directed by the *Army* Commander. Secondly, that the fighter governed the front and this fact required the centralisation of air power in the hands of an airman to exploit its flexibility. For instance, fighters must not be used as local umbrellas over a static front because this would leave the Luftewaffe free to hammer airfields, rear areas and supply lines. Thirdly, that air superiority must be sought and continually maintained both to permit the orderly concentration of friendly forces and their build-up of supplies and to impede that orderly concentration and build-up by enemy forces. If enemy movement could be restricted to the hours of darkness, *unescorted* bombing (by a force too small and vulnerable to risk unescorted in daylight) became possible. And fourthly, that the battlefield be isolated, as far as possible, by destroying access to it — whether by road, bridge, rail way, river, canal or port — for troops or supplies.

These principles did not specify what degree (if any) of close air support the soldier could expect. As Sir Kenneth Cross has written, some soldiers said: 'if you can keep the enemy air off our backs, that's all we ask; we can cope with the rest.' Until a late stage in the Mediterranean War, it was the most that could even be attempted. It was also, as Cross observed, wishful thinking on the soldiers' part — given the expertise of their German opponents. Later, as Allied air power increased and enemy air power declined, 'protecting backs' would be regarded as the very least that should be done. After victory in Tunisia, air power would sometimes be expected to substitute for ground action. To do so, it would need specially-designed fighter-bombers and more rapid and accurate communications systems between air and ground units than were available in the

North African and Tunisian campaigns.

The good effect of Coningham's Tripoli speech was increased by Leigh-Mallory's visit to Tunisia in March-April 1943. As head of Fighter Command, he went there to study the air organisation with future operations across the Channel in mind. Leigh-Mallory's report to Portal, warmly commending the organisation of Coningham's command as excellent both in operations and in fostering good relations with other services, British and American, was well received. It led to the Air Ministry revamping Army Cooperation Command into the Second Tactical Air Force (Coningham's being the first) in June 1943. To take over that command, once a Channel crossing emerged as a realistic prospect, would become Coningham's ambition.

Kuter took with him to Washington on 13 May 1943 a report that was in fact an indictment of the handling of air power during the Tunisian Campaign before the re-organisation in February. Until then, American doctrine was expressed in a Field Manual 31-35 which cast aviation in a defensive role with the neutralising of enemy air power as a secondary task. For example, the manual did not even mention airfields among suitable targets for air strikes. This doctrine ran counter to what air officers had been learning at the Air Corps Tactical School, where the faculty preached unity of command and concentration of forces for offensive action to attain that first priority, air superiority. 'Although Coningham was therefore preaching to at least some converts in Tunisia, he was supporting what they believed from personal experience, backed by the prestige of success. Kuter had a new manual written, FM 100-20 which became US War Department policy on 21 July 1943. As General William Momyer, USAF, has written, that manual is 'the emancipation proclamation' of tactical air power in the United States. Communications links and procedures for setting priorities in answering calls for air support had still to be worked out, but the doctrine made possible, in the words of two eminent American historians, 'one of the most effective collaborations known to military history.'

Only in the final stages of that collaboration did air superiority become air *supremacy* as the valiant Luftwaffe ran out of pilots and petrol. Given supremacy, as in Desert Storm, aircraft can carry out accurate bombing of the battlefield, supply lines and access routes, around the clock — preventing enemy sleep as well as movement. But as for close air support, ground fire remains as dangerous as ever, even from what one pilot called a 'prehistoric' curtain of cannon and tracer put up by flak batteries. 'I never imagined there could be that much ground fire', said another pilot. Quite a few BE2c and Kittyhawk veterans of earlier desert storms, hogging the bar in that Great Mess in the Sky, will have smiled to hear such words.

I began with the Mediterranean War's most famous commander and will now end with another word from Rommel to help us keep 'commanders and command systems' in their proper perspective. At the proudest moment of his amazing career in North Africa, the moment in June 1942 when he captured Tobruk, the achievement which earned him a Field Marshal's baton, Rommel said: 'You know, it's not just leadership that produces a triumph like this. You've got to have troops who will accept every imposition you put upon them — deprivation, hardship, combat and even death. I owe everything to my soldiers.'

Chairman

We have been privileged to hear yet another speaker with a light touch but a very serious message, this time on the importance of the personalities involved, and showing how fortunate the Allies were in the commanders they had.

Author, Vincent Orange and Marshal of the Royal Air Force, Sir Michael Beetham, President RAF Historical Society.

Air Marshal Sir Frederick Sowrey, Chairman RAF Historical Society, with (l-r) Major Craig Seeber (USAF-Ex C-5 pilot), Wg Cdr Bruce Wynn (RAF Engineer Officer), Lt Cdr 'PD' Weber (USN – F14 'Nav').

Air Commodore Henry Probert, RAF Historical Society Programmes Sub Committee Chairman

Group Captain Ian Madelin, Head of Air Historical Branch and Derek Wood, Editor of RAF Historical Society 'Proceedings'

48 THE END OF THE BEGINNING

Staff College students W/Cdr Helen Randal, S/L Chris Carver with Dr Horst Boog, Luftwaffe historian, and John Terraine, historian

Air Chief Marshal Sir Michael Armitage with Air Commodore R. H. Gould, Depty Commandant Staff College

THE END OF THE BEGINNING 49

Desert Commanders

Sqdn Ldr acting Group Captain "Bing" Cross with Flt Lt acting Wg Cdr Fred Rosier, Nov. 1941. "Fred had been missing for 3 days and walked home through a German Armoured Division. We were laughing because the opinion in the wing was that the enemy reckoned he was more use to them when working with us than he would be as a POW!"

Air Chief Marshals Sir Kenneth Cross and Sir Frederick Rosier, March 1992. "To misquote a well known Royal Air Force song — There is promotion this side of the ocean."

8. Digest of the Group Discussions

After the formal presentations, those attending the seminar divided into discussion groups where the various issues raised could be considered in more detail and the recollections of those involved in the Mediterranean campaigns could be given. Each group was chaired by a member of the College Directing Staff and included military participants air historians, Bracknell staff and students and other serving officers.

The proceedings were all recorded and subsequently transcribed. A small editorial team then compiled a Digest of what appeared to be the most significant contributions. This Digest is reproduced below.

While every effort has been made to ensure that all statements included are accurately reported, the original transcription was not always easy. Thus, if the occasional error does appear, the editorial team can only apologise.

EDITORIAL TEAM
Mr. Sebastian Cox
Mr. Cecil James
Group Captain Ian Madelin
Air Commodore Henry Probert
Mr. Tony Richardson
Group Captain Andrew Thompson
Group Captain Geoffrey Thorburn
Mr. Derek Wood

A)

Flight Lieutenant Winsland started with a personal reminiscence. Flying a Hurricane to find a new landing ground for the squadron he was not equipped for night flying and overstayed time on search. He landed in the desert for the night and had a flat battery next morning; he walked and was picked up. He went back with a vehicle after four days, started the Hurricane and flew to base. The Hurricane was behind enemy lines undiscovered for four days.

Professor Wiseman I was sent out from the planning group that included Air Ministry Intelligence, working with Eisenhower on Operation Torch. I was sent to Gibraltar with maps and plans of this dangerous episode and had the problem of briefing the first squadron flying from Gib to land at Algiers, Maison Blanche. You will remember the now quite famous story of one of my Intelligence Officers there being refused permission for the aircraft to land so he ripped off his white shirt to make the necessary white cross to enable our people to land.

Memory of those days was changing air command structure whilst we were on the road. We were Eastern Air Command for a while, then North West Africa Tactical Air Force. Our main weakness was that no-one from the Desert Air Force came to give us their experience of supporting the army. My main task was dealing with the commanders with this Ultra secret operation. I had a mobile signals support unit from the UK and I had to interpret this information for the commanders who were in the know. I was not given the information as to which commanders were in the know and thus which I could talk to. Quite a major problem which changed rapidly later when we became the Mediterranean Allied Tactical Air Force when I then had to supply Mary Coningham. The secret of the air/army co-operation at that time was, in my judgement, the closeness of the commanders. They lived alongside each other's caravans, an idea copied from the western desert.

Mary Coningham, whom I had the privilege to work alongside, was very senior, he would always listen and then he encouraged me to go out and talk to the field intelligence officers, and in the army as well. In my briefings I always had to be careful, saying to myself "Did I get that from Ultra?" and then being circumspect.

As an example of this: I was once giving my daily report, Alex was there, Carl Spaatz, Monty, etc. quite an interesting experience seeing all these in daily conference and I reported that USAF B-52s had no hits at all on Palermo. The importance of intelligence is that it tells you the truth it knows. At this Carl Spaatz jumped up and said "How dare you say that, young man". I didn't know what to do, so I sat down behind George Beamish to whom I also reported, and watched the ripples on the back of his neck. Alex put his hand on Carl Spaatz's arm an said, "Don't worry, Carl, it's only what the Germans say". After that wherever I went I was greeted with "How dare you, young man".

ACM Sir Kenneth Cross Ultra in the Med was really ace. With no land lines, everything had to go over the air and Bletchley got the complete picture. The one theatre in which it was 100%, if anything can be 100%. When we had kicked the Germans out of Africa, I was transferred to Coastal Command and the force was lined up at Bizerta to sink the remaining Italian fleet which was at Genoa. In the meantime, we were to attack shipping coming down from Naples to Palermo; it was money for jam, the easiest thing that has ever been done, almost entirely on Ultra.

Dennis Richards agreed and pointed out that the last tanker Rommel was trying to get across to Tobruk was picked up from Ultra, while *Flt Lt Wiseman* remarked that Hut 3 at Bletchley supplied him with the complete order of battle and its changes, while his army colleagues had all the questions of rations and fuel supplies up to date.

Wg Cdr Allen asked whether from the intelligence standpoint, we gave any disinformation and was it given serious consideration at that time Prof. Wiseman replied that Ultra was only one source but that we did get quite a lot of disinformation from the Germans.

Derek Wood There were a large number of recce flights after an Ultra note on a convoy in order to make it appear that this was where the intelligence came from.

ACM Cross I had strict instructions that we were never allowed to strike on Ultra information alone, we always had to be covered by reconnaissance, but it was just too easy. Prior to Alamein, we got the impression from Ultra that the Germans were the most awful liars in their reports back to Berlin.

In answer to a question about when the breakthrough in Army-Air cooperation took place, *Dennis Richards* said that Tedder told him that it was with the arrival of Montgomery. He said Montgomery was the first chap who was prepared to study the air forces' own communications and then put someone up there alongside.

Sqdn. Ldr. Lex, Nigerian Air Force My question is related to the ferrying from West Africa to Cairo and related navigational problems. Even now with advanced nav aids we have problems with the dust haze. With known engine failures at the end of the ferry and the nav problems, how did you manage?

ACM Cross When I survived the sinking of "Glorious", I went to the Air Ministry and was posted to Egypt. Asking how I was going, they said you are going in HMS Furious. With the Glorious and Courageous being sunk, I did not feel this to be a good thing and thought about third time lucky. We were lucky not to be sunk as we ran into the Hipper but the weather was bad and we escaped; when we got off Takoradi, the captain wanted to put us off but I resisted. He said can't you navigate and I said no, all we have is a watch and a compass and when we hit the coast we shall be low on fuel and wouldn't know which way to turn. He said how near do you want to be and, being a practical sort of chap, I said near enough to see it. We were navigated across with a Blenheim and I was surprised how good the weather was in January. We were fortunate in not having any engine problems in my lot. The Blenheims used DR and astro to navigate, they'd got nothing else.

I had said to the 40 pilots, specially selected experienced pilots from Fighter Command on whom I checked, to find one with 15 hours on Hurricanes facing this 3,000 mile jaunt, that I would give them a bottle of Champagne on arrival, I think 38 made it.

Dennis Richards There is an interesting historical point arises in 1942 when retreating to Egypt. One of the very few occasions during the war when, despite us having air superiority, the army was still retreating. Partly due to our not knowing how to use our superiority effectively and partly because the army was not controlling its own units.

Anon Also because there was a breakdown of command in the army and also a breakdown in morale.

Major Maxi The army didn't know what it could do itself half the time. We had a great problem in getting everybody used to the armour, let alone worrying about what the RAF did. For years we could not get a proper doctrine of co-operation between the arms; it wasn't until after Alamein that we got our act together. We were all for you lot, you gave us good reconnaissance and information.

Dennis Richards took slight issue with John Terraine's view that the RAF overseas was concerned most of the time with co-operating with the army. They had an Army Cooperation Group, later promoted to a Command and an Air Component which was sent out with the Expeditionary Force. People like Leigh-Mallory had spent their lives on Army co-operation business. He thought that the air force did think of army co-operation as one of their jobs but they had limited resources and they didn't want to apply their aircraft to jobs very close to the troops which they felt the the troops should be doing with their artillery.

ACM Cross I am so glad that you make this point as Maurice Dean is the nigger in the woodpile, saying in his book that we 'forgot' the army. A bit uncharitable, I feel. If we had put it all into army co-operation, old Stuffy would have lost the lot; at least we got that one right.

Anon Perhaps we could turn our attention to air superiority. How did we achieve that? Initially the 109 was so superior to the Hurricane, was it just a case of weight of numbers and how quickly did re-equipping take place?

Anon It was just the weight of numbers, we were flying a so called wing of a couple of squadrons loosely together. Every daylight hour concentrating up sun in an area where we knew the Germans were sensitive to what was happening on the ground. With the Hurricane 1's we didn't have any great slaughter, neither with the Tomahawks which were the best things that we had, Hurricane 2's only came along with the Crusader thing but, by the same token, the army didn't get beaten up by the Luftwaffe in that Crusader battle. I think we could probably claim to have air superiority but probably the best way to describe it was that we managed to distract the Luftwaffe from attacking the army.

Don't forget that, although we may well have been inferior to the 109, our stuff was a lot better than that which the Italians had. Compare performance between the CR42 and Hurricane or Tomahawk, there was very little in it, except that the CR42 was much more manoeuvrable.

Derek Wood I must admit that one of the things that I have never understood was this unwillingness in the United Kingdom, whilst suffering very heavy losses and doing nothing with Rhubarbs and things, sending masses of people to their deaths over Northern France. The actual battle, the Germans having gone to Russia, was being fought over North Africa. Now, how can you do this with Tomahawks and very early Hurricanes with very rough engines and the finish wasn't much better. When you fit them with filters and things, the performance goes right down all over the place. You haven't got 20 mm cannon. You really can go on and on and on, so why on earth wasn't a priority given to send Spitfires and something better than the Tomahawk? I have never been able to get to the bottom of this reluctance to send any sort of modern warplane outside the confines of the United Kingdom.

ACM Cross We were discussing this coming down the garden this morning. I think Fighter Command needed 53 squadrons for the safety of this country in the Battle of Britain time and they finished up later on with 97 squadrons in Fighter Command and we were still with Hurricane 1's and Tomahawks and it was the domination of Fighter Command over-all fighter policy in the UK — they completely took over from Air Ministry, the Director of Ops AD was just a liaison officer. They dictated the policy of the thing and they were very closely tied up with industry, Rolls-Royce particularly, and all this business of twin superchargers to go higher and higher, all really with great respect, to no purpose. They negated the long-range purpose and we suffered by having no Spitfires in North Africa. They talked about Spitfires coming across the Takoradi route but I never saw one. The first flight of Spitfires, that were given to the Poles, came in February 1942. This is a thing that is going to be written about one day.

Anon Could I, Air Marshal, and you would know. The Air Force commanders were so in touch down the chain of command that they were well aware that this was a matter often mentioned in the Command. I think that we ought to be fair to Mary Coningham in particular, who was always saying "If only I had some Spits" and this had gone right up to the top where it really was political.

Dennis Richards it seems fairly obvious but, at the same time, you have to think of what they were projecting at their highest level, the Russians were still hammering for a second front and in '42 they were making rather stupid things like Dieppe and then for a long time they thought that they were going to have a second front in '43 until after Casablanca so, at the top I think the thinking was, well we will try and establish air superiority over France and so on. They could, of course, have used them (Spitfires) much more effectively.

Derek Wood They didn't get the air superiority in Northern France because, of course, the Germans recreated the conditions that they had been defeated by with us in 1940.

ACM Cross They didn't do a damn thing; I mean the Scharnhorst and Gneisnau sailed up in broad daylight, they were supposed to own the air over the Channel. Good gracious me!

Gp Capt Ian Madelin asked if there was a logistic reason why they didn't put other types of aeroplane into the Middle East. To which *Dennis Richards* replied that once you start sending an air force overseas, it becomes a hell of a job because it's not just the aeroplanes but MU's, etc. and having chaps there trained to service them.

One of the group then asked what about us being chivvied around the desert by 109's; how could they possibly sit in King Charles Street and say they couldn't deal with 190's and things without Spitfires V's and IX's when all the time there we were with Hurricane I's trying to deal with 109 F's and G's.

Another participant replied to the question Were you not genuinely worried that you were technically outclassed? The answer was Yes, we were certainly worried but really we didn't know any better".

Anon You may have seen an obituary in the press for a splendid chap called Robin Johnstone, a Wing Commander in the desert. When he had finished his time in Hurricane I's, he came back to England and got into an RAF Mustang squadron. I had a letter from him whilst I was in Italy saying, "Here I am, 25,000 feet over Germany, taking over from an American Wing escorting B17's, with great military precision and they can't do a damn thing about it.

Major Maxi We certainly experienced this in 1944 in our fight against German tanks, against the Tiger and above all against the Panther. We were outgunned and, furthermore, we couldn't penetrate the front of the Panther with anything that we had and we were shit scared about this. We really were and it made people hold back.

Sqn Ldr Bill Hartree In all the to-ing and fro-ing across the desert, how did you keep the squadrons together, or perhaps you didn't bother? Did you try to keep the squadrons together as an entity?

ACM Cross Like glue, that was the thing, the squadrons, the fighting unit. We went to tremendous lengths to keep them together. If we had mucked about with that, and with inferior aeroplanes, I don't think that morale would have stood it.

Anon Did you take your engineers with it?

Anon Oh yes, that was the key thing.

Anon Did this split-up have an effect on you in the Gulf, to which the reply was, yes, I think it did.

*Major Max*i I wasn't here but I have talked to some of the army formations, particularly the fourth armoured brigade. Same thing, it did have an effect on morale. There was an uncertainty in people's minds as to whether they would get the performance that they required.

Air Cdre Baldwin This is a very important subject that we raise. Some of the people in this room, the next generation, will be faced with this. We are grasping this issue now with various readiness states. As we all know there is no direct threat at this stage and we have somehow got to give ourselves an intellectual background, an underpinning of the Royal Air Force for the next ten or twenty years and the squadron ethos is to me very important, one of the reasons why I am here today. There are gems coming out here, I only wish we had heard them perhaps two years ago in a seminar at this very place when we were down in the bunker influencing the construction of those units that were going out to Tabuk and various other places, we might have had a bit more sway in the way those were constructed.

One of the interesting things to me is that we have plenty of time, so it turns out. In the Gulf we had time to train and build up and yet we allowed ourselves to be sucked into this business. As you know, we went out there with well-defined categories of aircrew competence. We all knew what we were, Al, C2 and the first thing that happened, we redefined them. One of the most important lessons for me from the Gulf experience that we now have a responsibility to the next planning cycle, the next generation. It is desperately important when we heed the Air Marshal, look at his reaction straight away, it was inbred into him after 50 years, that we need to get the damned thing injected into our bloodstream.

Anon: Why did you lose sight of it?

Air Cdr Baldwin It was not that we lost sight of it but a range of reasons came into it. We were going into an unknown, sending a Tornado force into a world it had never been into before; it had not been designed or planned to go to before. The whole doctrine of our Air Force and the whole training pattern of the Air Force and in that aeroplane in particular. Also its predecessors since the end of the war had all been geared to a European way and a particular scenario. This was a new one, a different scenario and the commanders who went out there at the very beginning wanted the best people they could get, they knew they were going into a highly complex and dangerous position of long-range and night refuelling; they wanted very high skill levels, they didn't want training crews, they wanted guaranteed skill levels. We changed rules somewhat.

Wing Cdr Broadbent I don't want to spend too much time on this as it's not directly involved in the Mediterranean. Just to put it into context, the Air Commodore has just put the reasons why we ended up with what we did but as the commander in the field tried to command elements from five squadrons in my own detachment, it was far less than ideal. In peacetime I would expect to have one and a half crews available per aircraft of which at any one time about 12 would be combat ready. In the Gulf we quite properly chose to increase the manning ratio up to two crews per aircraft, ie. 24 crews. Clearly one squadron could not provide all 24 and it would have to be a minimum of two squadrons and the same applied to ground crews.

In fact, I had, at one brief moment, two other squadron commanders working for me, as it were, before one of them got killed on his first war mission and the other went off to run one of the new pieces of technology coming into theatre but I think you can clearly see, with two commands represented and five squadrons and three squadron commanders, then this is not the way to run the war and we were fortunate in this regard that it was a pretty one sided effort because if the pressure had been on, then the cracks might well have appeared. They didn't in this one; it was not going to be a feature as we were clearly not going to lose but, when the chips are down, that is where real morale is when you dip into it and you need to plumb the depths, if it's not there, then you've got it wrong and by that time it's far too late.

Major Maxi As an army officer going round RAF units quite a lot during my time in the service up to 1968 and dealing with quite a lot of these matters, we began to notice, particularly after the fierce squadron loyalties that we had always known before, it was fading away.

Air Cdr Baldwin The Royal Air Force squadron loyalties are as high now as they have ever been. Any of the older generation here would be very impressed with the squadron loyalties; they revere their standard as much as anyone ever has. Don't get a false impression. This was an unusual event that I am describing and our commanders handled it in a particular way for reasons that they thought at the time were very sensible. All that we can say with hindsight is that if we were doing it again we probably would not do it that way.

Dennis Richards Doesn't this depend to some extent on the sophistication of the technology that you have to deal with? For instance, if you take squadron coherence in the Battle of Britain, where there was a marvellous spirit between ground crews and the aircrew and they wished to preserve that, then when they found that they had to move squadrons constantly, taking them into rest and bringing them back again, that the actual movements of transporting the ground crew as well as the aircrew couldn't be done in time to set the thing up effectively and in the later stages of the battle the aircrews were going and at least half of the servicing was being done by chaps who were being kept back and not sent back to rest with their aircrew. In Bomber Command in the development of the base system finally, an awful lot of the major servicing was done at base rather than at the squadron. In the desert I think that they actually managed to make the squadrons cohere but there the technical thing was a bit less sophisticated than in Bomber Command say, towards the end of the war. One wonders if some element of this must be taken into account in planning.

Sqdn Ldr Stewart Having enjoyed, as a current course member here, all of the historical side this morning and indeed the last few minutes of discussion particularly, I think we finally come to the nub of it which for me is the lesson that there are no new lessons. We have learnt it all before and all you gentlemen who have served through all these different campaigns from this Gulf to that Gulf in North Africa, you have learnt exactly the same lessons which for me, as someone who hasn't been out there, I am impressed by the fact, as the Professor said, that history does keep repeating itself and all that has been discussed since we started this morning has relevance to us now. You talk of communications as just a quick example, Army to Air Force, ship to aircraft, and I hate to say it, but in my experience we still have problems when the chips are down. We talk of equipment and morale, we have considered ourselves in high tech terms poorly done by in certain bits of the Air Force but we made it all work. Notwithstanding superb morale, there are not many who have not looked longingly across the Atlantic and even into Europe for some of their stuff but I repeat the lesson that I have learnt well today is that there are no new lessons, we keep going round the same old wheel.

Anon Why did we lose sight?

Sqdn Ldr Stewart Why did we lose sight, as the question was put. Is it that if too many years go by in between conflicts, we completely flush through all our commanders. There aren't any last war campaign leaders around to say lead in the Gulf. Has it all gone? Where does it all go? Do our leaders each think that they know best, have a new idea that nobody else has thought of?

Anon I think the point was made this morning that all the hard learnt lessons of the First World War atrophied between the wars and we quite literally started from scratch taking us until 1942 to get back to where we were in something like 1917.

Anon I think one should be a little careful. There are new principles and techniques to be learnt as technology comes in and develops. One ought to be aware that there are new ideas and whilst the principles are there that laid down those foundations, technology will move on.

Wing Cdr Broadbent Could we continue this question of mobility of squadrons, a fairly new thing in 1942, do any participants at that time have recollections of any particular problems that were raised then?

ACM Cross Can you imagine the Middle East Air Force sitting there, Helwan, Heliopolis, etc. with squadrons which had no transport? The transport belonged to the station. It wasn't until the advent of Tommy Elmhurst in 1942 who said what about an establishment of transport for the squadrons. It really was a miracle that they weren't all caught on the ground. It is difficult to believe that it ever got out of the minds of the commanders that the aircrew can't go anywhere without the ground crew.

B)

John Terraine I am surprised nothing was said this morning about a paper issued in the Middle East in September 1941: "The Land/ Air Directive". Note, this was not a discussion paper; it was a "Directive". It was the result of a conference with reasonably high level army and air representatives and was an actual blueprint for land/air co-operation. It seemed to me when I was researching 'Right of the Line' that, in this field, for the whole of the rest of the war, it was simply a story of the adherence to (or non-adherence to) this document. So it is surprising it did not get any mention this morning. It was clearly a turning point in the whole development of this subject. There are those who would say that the oracle of this subject was Army Co-operation Command back in this country. I am absolutely sure it was not, and the very issuing of this document supports the point. What makes it even more surprising is that there is, still now, in the Air Historical Branch a monograph on this very subject which contains in detail all the work which was done with all the suitable diagrams to illustrate it, and I don't see how a study of this subject can advance very far without an awareness of that monograph. I would warmly recommend it should be reprinted, and issued to the appropriate Services in substantial quantities. What do you say to that IM?

Ian Madelin Well yes, it is a good idea. Unfortunately though, we (unlike the Americans) do not much use the word 'doctrine' and it is not an idea we are comfortable with. We are the arch pragmatists, and you can have books on 'doctrine' and nobody reads them. Or if they do, they don't make a connection between what they are reading about and what they're doing.

Robert Jackson (seeking John Terraine's views).

There was mention this morning of air/land co-operation in the First World War, in its variety of roles, but no mention of the German Schlachtflieger who developed this to a very fine art in 1917-18 and continued with it throughout the inter-war years, through the war in Spain, into the Second World War. Which is why they never lost the lessons.

John Terraine Yes, that sums it up. The Germans continued to operate in a continuum and we did not, which was a very dangerous state of affairs.

Gp Capt Bisdee What you say about the Germans is true, but they did not carry this through into the design of aircraft they used. The Ju 87 was the easiest aircraft to shoot down I have ever known and right up to the end of the war they were using aircraft not suited to their roles. All I would say is that the Germans learned the lesson, they applied it, but they never changed it.

Robert Jackson That is very true. We changed our tactics to suit the circumstances of the time. They continued to operate in the same old way, and they got stopped in the same old way.

Wg Cdr Dick Bonella Perhaps that is the key to it. On our side all we ever have is tactics. We change tactics, but there is no doctrine behind it. Tactics are merely something devised by a bright fellow on the spot to suit particular circumstances. A fundamental doctrine would say; "Here are the principles, now apply them" — and the tactics would fall out.

Robert Jackson returns to the matter of German ground-attack aircraft and says it was not correct that they did not have a suitable design. They never lost sight of the need for design and engineering applied to tac/air. There was, for example, the Henschel 123, which was very effective, and we had nothing like it. And the Henschel 129. Both optimised for ground attack. Until the Typhoon we had nothing like that. Perhaps though the aircraft were parcelled up in little bundles too much and not properly employed to a larger degree.

Col David James Presumably the German army was propelling the Luftwaffe in their direction, as a tactical air arm for them. Whereas here, with our brigade level exercises on Salisbury Plain, we weren't pushing this to anything like the same extent.

Robert Jackson Remember that Leigh-Mallory was a great exponent of this when he was at the Army Co-operation School in the '20s. He stuck his neck out a long way to bring home the importance of tac/air to the powers-that-be, and he was not appreciated for it. He did not return to this role until the Tactical Air Forces were formed in 1943. So what happened in between? Somebody must know what went wrong in this country.

Ian Madelin I'm not going to take up your point about "what went wrong in between", but I'd like to return to your previous point when you were mentioning the Luftwaffe's ground attack aircraft, to highlight the contrast you made. You said that we had 'nothing like that'. This is worth emphasising because it is not often realised. We had absolutely nothing like that. Looking back from now one imagines, let us say the Hurricane, doing ground attack, because that's what they eventually came to do, as did the Spitfire. But in the period we discussed this morning they didn't do ground attack. They were purely 'fighters', and the word then meant air defence fighters and that was their role. Air Marshal Rosier said this morning: "By El Alemein, certain aircraft (ie fighters) had been fitted to carry bombs" you see, It was only then that we started to use those aircraft for ground attack. When Air Marshal Cross was posted out to Egypt it was as someone with Fighter Command experience in order to set up a fighter defence organisation. None of the aircraft which we now know to have been suitable for this kind of work were doing this kind of work. It was left to the Blenheims and the light bombers.

And that has happened since. During the 50's there was a period of at least 6 years with fighters when we weren't putting rockets on them or using them for strafing. Air Marshal Cross who was flying fighters from about 1933, off and on right up to this period, didn't do any air to ground strafing at all until about 1943.

Maurice Harvey We need to put all this in perspective. We heard this morning from John Terraine that there was this emphasis between the wars on the doctrine of strategic bombing, at the expense of air/ground support. Remember though that the Germans, in 1934-35, toyed with the idea of doing the same thing, and did try to develop a strategic bomber themselves but found it was technically unachievable at that time. (Perhaps we should have come to the same conclusion?). Therefore they developed this ground/air doctrine, which was highly successful in Poland and in the Low Countries. But then they tried to use these very same aircraft for strategic bombing against this country in 1940 and they were just as unsuccessful in that as we were in trying to use our aircraft in the air/ground role. So I don't think we should necessarily say that we got it all wrong and they got it right.

Ian Madelin The difference is though that we did have the aircraft for the role — Hurricanes, and later, Spitfires and they didn't. I remember Air Marshal Cross telling me that the only time during gunnery camp in the '30s that they fired at the ground with the fighters was when they were using ground targets as a substitute for air-to-air targets (because there weren't many towed aerial targets available then). It was a sort of 'poor man's' attempt to do air-to-air training, but the aircraft would have been very suitable for air-to-ground.

Maurice Harvey But I think the whole emphasis up to 1940, say, had to be to use the fighters for the air defence of Great Britain. I don't think we had the time or the energy to think of anything else.

Ian Madelin. Perhaps. But there is also the factor we have been talking about today, namely, to what extent were we being blinkered?

Hugh Skillern There was some effective air support to the army in June 1940. It is little remembered and history gives the impression that for us the Battle of France ended at Dunkirk with the little ships coming back. There was the biggest land battle in history up to that time with four German army groups against four French army groups on the other side of the Somme. In the middle of that were two British Divisions. They had the sector from Abbeville to the Somme, some 40 miles, and they carried out attacks on the heights of Cambron where the Germany artillery was. The RAF flew big sorties in this combined Anglo/French attack. But communications were poor to nonexistent, whether between our own arms engaged on the ground, or from there back to the headquarters at Dieppe. The German air force and army were blended together, as one arm under the OKW.

Wg Cdr 'Cas' Capewell It seems to me that the first lessons we have to learn at the start of every conflict is to relearn the lessons we learnt in the last one. How can we make sure we don't forget. We've just been hearing how we designed aeroplanes with a certain role in mind and we forgot about other things. We have aircraft in service today, that were in the Gulf conflict, designed with one purpose in mind that could not do anything else and were almost wasted. How can we maintain our thinking so that we don't make these same mistakes, it would seem, time after time again?

John Terraine. I think that military history has a very definite role in this respect.

I was going to just raise the question of close support aircraft — 3 in particular. This is a question, not a statement and I am hoping you will be able to clear my own mind on this subject. The first aircraft is the Ju 87. It was a resounding success, both in Poland and in France in 1940, so much so that there was agitation in this country, spearheaded I think by Beaverbrook for us to start production of a version of our own. But the Air Ministry set its face firmly against it, and though they were wrong about a great many things at that time, they were not wrong about this. We were able to do all the things that the Ju 87 was supposed to do, but without incurring its hazards and its swift obsolescence. I admit that, until this morning I would have included the rocket-firing Typhoon as an example but I was told today by someone whose opinions I respect that it was an utter flop. So there is one case of the perils of custom-built aircraft.

Next, we've already heard mention of the Henschel which, I think, was a good aircraft, but surely the British equivalent was the Westland Lysander. It was much admired by almost everyone who flew it, but surely the joke about the Lysander was it was good at pretty much everything except the purpose for which it was designed.

Finally I'll throw in the Me 262. It was designed as a fighter, a jet fighter in advance of anything else at its time. But it was forced into the fighter bomber role, by the doctrine in the mind of Hitler.

So there are the three aircraft, I am not sure in my own mind what those case histories are telling us but I commend them to you for some consideration.

Gp Capt John Bisdee Well I think in fact the Typhoon was successful in the anti-tank role. The disaster the Germans suffered at the Falaise Gap was due in large measure to the work of the Typhoons, which was intended, I agree, as an air defence fighter but turned out to be an excellent ground-straffer. I don't think it was, in that role, a flop at all.

John Terraine I'm wide open on this, which is a new one on me. But the story I got this morning came from the Mortain experience — always quoted as making a new chapter in airpower history — was about a squadron of Typhoons attacking a mass of German tanks and firing off all their 96 rockets at them. Reconnaissance the next day showed 96 holes in the ground and the only damage was that a single German halftrack had had one of its tracks blown off.

Ian Madelin. I would not hold that against the aircraft which fired the rockets. It is more an overestimate — which one still encounters everywhere — of what aircraft can do against pin-point targets. Even when you are doing this kind of thing in training, in a leisurely way, flying academic patterns with no ground defences you count the results in terms of "miss distance", and taking the results of a squadron as a whole its average "miss distance" will be bigger than the size of the average tank. You may think we are now straying on to a different subject but it is an issue which does arise in this campaign, namely: What can the air best do for the ground? A soldier may well reply: "Take out tanks." The trouble is one is tempted to try to rise to the occasion, but if we were being sensible we'd say that we were not very good at taking out tanks. We are nothing like as good as your anti-tank weapons which are day/night, all-weather, more responsive, and accurate. On the other hand there are things which we can do which you can't do. So you should not hold that against the Typhoon. You could do a similar calculation today, with the Jaguar say, and today's rockets, but you'd still find that to give yourself a better than 50% chance of knocking out one tank you may need a lot of aeroplanes.

John Sweetman. A comment on the Me 262 which was, as you say due to a quite emotional reaction of Hitler to the attacks on the German homeland. He said, if the fighters can't defend against this they might as well be turned into bombers. What we are really getting at here though is the political perceptions of the moment as to what the armed forces will require in the future. The trend in the '20s and '30s, stemming from Trenchard, was for an independent force of bombers to attack the enemy homeland, with a force of fighters to prevent the enemy doing that to you, and the RAF went along with that. What we should be doing now is looking at the lessons of the Gulf War to see what we should be doing for the future in relation to the political culture of the time.

Anon We have just come out of a war which no one could have foreseen and the first thing we do after that is start cutting down. The big problem we have is knowing how to persuade politicians that the job we have to do really is important.

John Terraine Yes, the point that emerges, with startling clarity, from both the Falklands and from the Gulf, is that wars are absolutely unpredictable. You never know what they are going to arise out of. All you can know is that they do arise. That is a political matter.

Chairman That's a very valid point. Note that we are far into an election campaign but defence hasn't even been mentioned yet. For many years now 80% of our thoughts and resources have been devoted to the Central Region. Now we are going to have to think globally, and that may mean that we shall have to be changing some of our kit, and given the long lead times entailed, if we are going to do that we would need to think quickly and start now.

Neil (Cromarty?) We have heard a lot today about lessons being forgotten but I wonder how much of this happens because of a personality clash. What does the panel think?

John Terraine One thing that frightens me most today, every time I open my newspaper, is the parallel between today and the attitudes of the '20's, and while we are talking about doctrine and dogma let us not leave out the 'anti-war' dogma. There is that extraordinary alliance between economists, pacifists, internationalists and various other kinds of people who created the 'political correctness' of the '20's which astonishingly resembles the political correctness of today. And that absolutely frightens the daylights out of me. And where history *ought* to come in, if it is allowed half a chance is to enable people to spot these alarming resemblances, to realise what may be in store for them if they don't do something about it.

(There follows a lengthy discussion about the origins of the RAF and strategic bombing policy until the questioner brings the matter to the desert war, and the extent to which personality clashes may have contributed to the loss of lessons there).

Ian Madelin It had a lot to do with it but not necessarily because they didn't get on with each other but because, as we've said, there was no doctrine so there was no foundation on which to build, and therefore nothing continuing or lasting. What happened is you would get a relationship between the airman and the soldier — the commanders — and they would work this out, in the absence of any doctrine. Then one or other of them would get posted — it was generally the soldier, and the airman would have to start again with the new man.

I'd like to go back though to the question as to what we can do about this? I don't think there is any easy answer, but I'd like to think that days like this one might contribute to it, because the way to start is to have some realisation of it. Otherwise we'll just keep on forgetting. I'd like to stress a point made earlier by John Terraine with a quote from Andrew Humphrey, a great Chief of the Air Staff. Addressing our College of Air Warfare he said: "If there is another war there is only one thing you can be sure about — that it is more likely to be different from than similar to, anything you imagined it would be".

There was a time, for example, during the '50's when for almost a decade our fighter squadrons did no land/air operations at all. It was because the great threat was the Soviet Union and that was going to be a nuclear war so what was going to be the point of ground straffing etc if that happened? So it was thrown out of the window. Yet it was obvious to most of the theorists at the time that the one thing that was not going to happen was a strategic nuclear exchange, but that what we should look out for instead — to use an expression which came into use at that time — were 'limited wars'. And what we have been having ever since then has been a series of 'limited wars'. Yet although this prospect was staring us in the face we disregarded it altogether.

Sqn Ldr Chris Harper This is a new question. I am having some difficulty here in identifying exactly what are these "lessons" which we should get out of this Mediterranean conflict, because it seems to me they didn't do too badly. I became aware of this as a theme of this seminar as today approached, but now I am unclear about it. We've heard today about fantastic levels of flexibility being displayed. So despite doctrine or the lack of it we seemed to have the right type of leaders and commanders who were using their aircraft in the right ways and doing the right things. Could I have some views on that?

Ian Madelin It is a very good question. And you are quite right; there has been a lot of talk about lessons, and lessons being learned, and lessons being forgotten. So it is a fair question. What is the lesson? There were a few things we heard about this morning which may indicate the answer.

There was the point when we had in the desert a large air force, ready, and waiting to support the army but not being called upon. It was Montgomery who got the point. The 'air' had been looked upon as an extension of the army's organic weapons and you used it in the same way — without understanding the characteristics of the 'air' weapon itself. Soldiers clearly understand the difference of characteristics between a howitzer and an anti-tank gun and a bren and a pistol, and you match each to what you are using it for. But they don't understand that the 'air' weapon has characteristics too which fit it superbly for some things but it is very ill-used for others. If you approach this from the soldiers' point of view the 'air' is in fact ill-suited for most of the things which the army's weapons can do, but it is not ill-suited for the sorts of things an airman would do, and if you don't ask the airman you will end up either badly misusing your air assets, or not using them at all. This point was emphasised toward the end of this morning by Air Marshal Cross who said: "Don't ask us what to do and don't tell us what to do, but you tell us what you want to do and we'll tell you how best we can help you". There was quite a long period when we could have created havoc for a German retreat but we weren't being used and we were waiting to be asked. That is the lesson, or to put it in Montgomery's words: "There isn't an air plan, and an army plan, there is *one* plan — air and army working together".

Lt Col Brian Eady CF Why did it take so long for army to get together with air force in the desert, and for this lesson to get across?

John Terraine In my view, quite frankly, it was because the army didn't know what it was about. You've done a lot of breast-beating today about the iniquities of the RAF, but it wasn't until Montgomery got there that the army began to get its business straight. Until then they clove desperately to one view, which was that you must not, at any cost, do anything which might resemble what went on between 1914 and 1918, even if that meant winning. Even winning wasn't on if you did it that way. It wasn't until Montgomery put the army back on to the system for which it had been organised, and restored artillery to its proper role in battle that you could then move on to any coherent plan for air co-operation. Up till then the weak element in the plans was always the army. And every time they lost a battle they went scrambling back into Egypt and everything had to start again. But this is a tri-Service matter, this forgetting or rejecting lessons from the past, and all were equally to blame. The navy for example rejected every lesson of anti-submarine warfare which it had learned between 1916 and 1918.

(Chairman — speaks in support, quoting army tactics pre and post-Montgomery).

Wg Cdr Dick Bonella If I could follow a point made by both Ian

Madelin and John Terraine about army and air working together, what about the US Army? They had their own air. Were they better placed, or worse, as a result?

Maurice Harvey Although in theory they were part of the same organisation in fact the Army Air Force had operated autonomously since about at least 1936.

Dick Bonella Yes but they still resented bitterly this Army connection and wanted to be completely separate like the RAF so there must have been some level of control there or they wouldn't have wanted to be free of it.

Ian Madelin Well the connection was really institutional not strategic or tactical, and that is one thing we have not discussed so far, namely the extent to which institutional rivalries can shape strategy and tactics, independently of the actual military needs of the time. For example, the USAAF's eagerness to participate in the strategic bombing campaign had a lot to do with carving out a role for itself which had nothing to do with what the army did. In fact there was tremendous bad blood between the 'army/army generals' and the 'air/army generals' dating back to the time of Billie Mitchell. So the fact that the USAAF was part of the army did not mean that it functioned as the army's tactical air arm along the German pattern. On the contrary, they were trying to show that they were separate.

Gp Capt Bisdee It fascinated me to talk last year to American pilots who were in the Gulf to see how radically the whole business has changed. There wasn't the close contact between the ground armies which we saw in the desert, in Italy, and in our war. The ranges were much greater and it was the air which took on the enemy army with our own army going in at the end, to finish it off in 3 days.

Chairman (Army!) Yes but I think we have to be careful about extrapolating the lessons of the Desert War to the Gulf War, which is a whole subject in itself. All I would say, having listened to the presentations of this morning, is that with all of the technology now at our disposal we are not as far ahead as we ought to be. We still have 'blue on blue' accidents, we don't have a battlefield-wide IFF system which takes in both land and air, and the army is sorely underequipped with organic air-defence systems.

John Terraine. Yes, in the Desert, the Germans always excelled us with their air defence systems, fully mobile and fully integrated.

C)

AM Sir Patrick Dunn July 40 took over 80 Sqn Gladiators. Excellent training evident so little to be done. Objective to achieve air superiority over IAF — even with Gladiators not too difficult. Difficult to find and catch them — their initial success against us 4 out of 4 shot down (one of the two survivors, Sir Peter Wykeham). When we managed to get the Italians in the open we normally came out on top and from July to Dec 1940 we invariably had to hunt them out. Main battle started on 9 Dec when the army advanced and we had some success against their SM 79s and the escorting fighters. The army successfully drove them out of Egypt and through Libya to Cyrenaica.

So much for my part in the early stages of the war. By that time we had Hurricanes — a good aeroplane particularly when, if out of ammunition, one had to make a run for home. Difficult to hit the CR42s, manoeuvrable as Gladiators in close combat. When the IAF had been defeated we were tasked with ground attack operations in support of the army. Uncertainty about targets, no organisation for identifying them — "old boy" system. Plenty of soft-skinned vehicles to attack, though some reservation about such targets and time came when the army couldn't tell us where they were and the element of doubt crept in — were they our own? Silenced us for a while and I suppose that was my first lesson.

The Hurricane was not very manoeuvrable in comparison with the Macchi 202 or a Regiano. Much army support arranged between RAF and Army pre-war acquaintances and somewhat amateurish.

Sqn Ldr Mervyn Mills Camp Commandant during AM Coningham's time when at La Marsa just outside Tunis, the planning of the Sicily and Italian Campaigns were underway. I remained with the TAF throughout these campaigns and the capture of Corsica, ending up in Florence at the end of the war. Reflecting back and, indeed, even at the time felt the awe of experiencing historical events and personalities. My contribution today must be based on awareness of those men who were to have such an influence upon the development of land/air warfare techniques — more even than the improved aircraft that came. (Narrator with AHB on the campaign after the war). Viewed Coningham as a leader possessing not only great ability but also genius. Ably supported by the SASO, Beamish, who was a most able tactician.

Mr. R. C. Hurst A humble WOp/AG from 1940 and arrived at Malta on 1 May 1942 and in the 12 days there the airfield was attacked 61 times. On to Cairo but sent back to UK to convert to Liberators. Back to ME starting bomber operations with 178 Sqn. Later transferred to 148 Sqn which was engaged in support of guerrilla activities in the Balkans. Not shot at much but a hazardous terrain made ops uncomfortable for low-level drops. Use of Mk 1 Liberators not equipped with superchargers and self-sealing tanks, often carrying thin-walled sea mines with 1000 lbs high explosive. Lack of spares, much cannibalising and engineer ingenuity needed. After 300 hours such flying was returned to UK to be an instructor, lived happy ever after.

Prof. Bond A military historian and certainly not a specialist in today's topic, he never expected to speak, but happy to make a few points to open up discussion. First point concerned the poor state of Army/RAF inter-war relations — an unhelpful background to the campaign being considered today. Difficult to apportion blame but, as John Terraine pointed out, the RAF had had to fight for its very existence for many years during which it developed a strong commitment to strategic bombing. Some individuals aware of need for army co operation, Sir John Slessor for one, but despite the period of rearmament when war came the RAF was inadequately equipped for such operations and the combination of poor facilities, poor co-operation and the fast-moving nature of the conflict resulted in the disaster of the Battle of France. Sir Christopher Foxley-Norris has given us a vivid picture in his biography "Lighter Shade of Blue" of an airman's experiences of how bad things were at that time. Not perhaps entirely relevant to today's discussion but a useful backcloth.

Secondly, and to inject a rather more critical note reference to Col Charles Carrington's experiences as a liaison officer with Bomber Command who reflected that despite all the improvements in co-operation that were achieved it still fell far short of perfection by the time of the Normandy landings — incidences of tragic confusion over the bomb line and failure of ground/air communications. Had the lessons learned in the Desert War not resulted in more effective harmonisation (maybe the circumstances were different) or, as John Terraine pointed out that lessons once learned had been forgotten again and new personnel had to learn them. Possibly, the "barons" of Bomber Command were still not receptive to the Army's needs. In raising these contentious points he hoped to stimulate discussion and, in this connection, took issue with the comment that it wasn't up to the Army to tell the airman what he had to do but for the air to say what was possible; as an objective historian he would like to think that it was not a case of one Service telling the other what to do but of getting together in combined headquarters to work out a genuine joint command.

Sqn Ldr T. Almond Agreeing that we sometimes appeared to have forgotten the lessons of World War One and concentrated on strategic bombing which, if anything, had been the least noteworthy of the air force successes. In the North African campaign there were even closer lessons and disparities — why, for example, did Auchinlek separate the recently-formed joint army/air headquarters established by Collishaw. Similarly, when Operation TORCH started the Americans and combined forces appear to have learned nothing from Tedder's experiences. Were there underlying reasons for such disregard for precedent? Force of circumstances, the lapse of time, was the Air Force too mobile?

AM Dunn Very difficult to establish why co-operation doesn't occur. Very friendly relations in Western Desert in the early days on a personal level but this not mirrored in the system generally — badly equipped to maintain communications; armoured car running over field telephone wires would cut communications inevitably causing delay. Nevertheless, there was a joint HQ (201 or 202 Gp) in which Collishaw had his opposite numbers. He was a great commander against the Italians — whose inter-Service co-operation was, if anything, worse than ours — and fighting, thus, on parallel lines. But we never got really hot targets such as troop or vehicle concentrations and had to search ourselves because the bomb-line was so far back — we were 50 miles behind it and the Italians were similarly deployed — and so we went out to attack targets of opportunity. Later on, the bomb-line got closer and such tactics became more difficult and when we were driven back almost to Alexandria things really had to be tightened up and communications firmly established. But there were breakdowns which were not wilful but a fact of operational life.

Gp Capt Thorburn Criticisms of lack of co-operation may well have arisen because of the lack of the right equipment and the low priority accorded to close support facilities during peacetime. This gave rise to the view that lessons were constantly being re-learned and he cited as an example the post 1945 experience when, despite the tremendous strides made in the development of joint tactics during the war, they were quickly dissipated in the post-war years and this occurred largely because of financial pressures which forced each Service to preserve its own interests. We see the whittling away of tactical facilities such as the loss of mobile radars, ranges and alternative airfields so that the training environment in which co-operation was best fostered was threatened. Inevitably, the lessons of tactical co-operation would have later to be re-learned.

Wg Cdr Lewis But surely in the post-war world we lost sight of lessons primarily because of concentrations on nuclear deterrence and the tactical concept was indeed suppressed by the view that there wouldn't be a tactical war. Over the years we changed that posture to graduated response and caused us to think tactically again. Whilst the Treasury may have played its part, concepts were influenced by strategy on a grand scale.

Gp Capt Thorburn Whilst this was undoubtedly highly important the consequence was the gradual elimination of facilities in which the retention of concepts of tactical co-operation were fostered — a loss which didn't result from positive policy but from necessary economies.

Prof. Bond The strength of bombing doctrine in the inter-war period had certainly influenced strategy and in the war in Europe we saw continuing tension between the needs of the Army and the Navy and Harris's mission of bombing Germany. In the Mediterranean theatre, however, there were individuals who were not so committed and there weren't major strategic targets and so those causes of conflict were not present. Was it the theatre and the nature of the war being fought there that fostered the co-operation we heard about this morning?

Mr. Lacey-Johnson Following up point about the loss of techniques developed during the war. Not all the significant units disappeared, the Air Support Signals Units, for example, existed until quite recently. As a former Army man he confessed to have smarted at the comment that the ground forces often didn't know where the enemy was or, on occasion, even their own forces. In 1941, that we were in the embryonic stages of photographic reconnaissance was not commented on during the morning's presentations and there was no explanation of how it subsequently developed in 1942/3.

AM Dunn A PR facility existed from the earliest stage but the results were not available until a couple of days after being taken — and then not in photographic, but statement form. That the targets were still there and subsequently attacked successfully was a comment on the opposition. We should never have been permitted such opportunities. However, by 1942 the PR process had been speeded up.

Tony Jutsum Enquired about the stage at which visual Control Post officers were introduced — they were tour expired fighter bomber pilots who were controlling close support ops and techniques were well developed during the Italian, European and Burma campaigns.

AM Dunn Not aware of live voice controllers in the Western Desert though they may have been available during the Operation TORCH campaign, and when serving as an Air Ministry staff officer and involved in the preparation of operational summaries could not recall reference to their employment. But he was convinced that the prime mover in initiating their introduction was Gordon Finlayson but could not put a date on it. He wished to remedy any impression that co-operation was poor — it wasn't but the machinery to ensure that it was good wasn't there. He endorsed the point made about Treasury control which so curtailed acquisition of other than the most vital equipment; a concomitant was the absence of associated techniques. Laying the law down to Treasury experts was no easy matter — they debated well but Air Marshals, who knew what they wanted, were no match for them in debate at that time.

Sqn Ldr Almond Following a point made by Prof Bond about the type of target and resource management, his impression was that there was a very significant protectionism environment between the various Commands. Bomber Command's total preoccupation with striking the heart of Germany and insisting on priority of resources to achieve the task; Coastal Command on stretched resources in contrast, and North Africa even lower in the pecking order. It wasn't so obviously a strategic campaign and it was not so much the type of target as the type of resource available which explains why a major bombing concept didn't dominate that campaign.

Prof. Bond Commented that it was perhaps dangerous if we take too short a view by looking at just one campaign. We should develop the point about what went on in the inter-war period with three Service ministries developing their separate strategies — the Army, imperial garrisoning, the Navy, its pre-occupation with the Far East and the RAF developing a very strong strategic bombing mentality, each of which the Treasury was well aware of and used the powerful hand of divide and rule. Given this, it was no surprise that the development of the spirit of co-operation took so long — getting the mental attitude first and then developing the material, it was always going to be 1942/3 before the essential joint co-operation would emerge. We need, therefore, to cast our minds back beyond 1941 to fully understand the struggle to develop that co-operation.

AM Dunn Agreeing, he recalled how important it was to the RAF to assume the air control of mandated territories in Iraq and Palestine, which helped to consolidate its independence because it showed how effectively it could do the job. However, when it came to 1939-45 there was nothing that the Service required that couldn't have been provided years before had the money been made available. But the Army and Navy in all sincerity didn't believe the RAF could achieve what it claimed it could do and, indeed, it couldn't initially because it did not have that equipment.

Mr. P. W. Large A member of 22 Army Co-operation Unit which, strangely, was in Fighter Command and which included seconded Army pilots. That unit felt very close to Army colleagues and went to France in early days of war but somehow that spirit didn't persist after the formation of Army Cooperation Command. As the campaign progressed, however, we were confident that co-operation with the ground forces was good.

AM Dunn In response to a question about enemy defences, observed that Italian airfields were not well defended despite ample AA resources. Control was poor but the position changed dramatically when the Luftwaffe arrived. Such attacks would normally be made by a flight of four aircraft rather than a squadron or wing.

AVM Oulton Resources essential to the achievement of effective close support were not initially available and Army co-operation had low priority, even in terms of personnel, for the best quality pilots went to Fighter Command, Bomber got the pick of the remainder and Army Co-operation the rest. Nevertheless, in 1936, an experiment under Sqn Ldr MacDonald with Dowding's support involving a two squadron bomber attack on UK succeeded in getting through unintercepted and seemed to confirm Air Ministry's belief in the strategic bombing concept. Coupled with that there was a noticeable coolness in the attitude of many influential Army officers to those in Light Blue for an aeroplane did not rate alongside the horse. Entrenched attitudes were to take a very long time to break down and he held great store by the current dedication to joint training at staff colleges and the resultant widening of understanding of each others disciplines. Turning to events in 1941 with limited resources and morale at a low ebb the only way in which the nation could be seen to be going on to the offensive was by the use of Bomber Command and Air Marshal Harris did the job he was given to the best of his ability — it wasn't his fault that someone told him to do the wrong job. Dowding similarly, saw his task as to defend the UK and not that of sending more of his aircraft to France. People may protest about a task but must nevertheless carry it out. Success in W Africa would have been of no avail if defeat in the UK had occurred and so the allocation of resources to these two theatres among numerous others was very difficult and an unenviable task. Collishaw showed the importance of getting all elements together to communicate with each other and resolve how best to assist each other in the common cause, each element being vital to the others.

Lt Cdr Holmes Felt that AVM Oulton had understated the degree of inter-Service training and co-operation that now existed — it was far wider than exchange at the staff college level and extended into the field of doctrine in the form of Allied Tactical Publications. A far better picture.

AVM Oulton Wouldn't disagree, but had to emphasise that as resources became scarcer so the tendency to concentrate on one's own job and that is the situation that must be guarded against and thank goodness the situation is as you describe. The danger is that progressive cuts in the defence budgets will make such liaison increasingly difficult to maintain, but it is essential that we do so.

Mr. Lewis Had no experience of the W African campaign but was for two years PA to Sir Keith Park in SE Asia and there it was clear that many of the commanders had Western Desert experience and there was utmost co-operation. Was it the influence of Mountbatten as Supreme Commander or was there another reason?

Tony Jutsum It was a fact that Slim and the air commander, Vincent, got on extremely well.

AM Dunn I hope I conveyed the point that the desire to co-operate was there but it was the machinery that was lacking or primitive and so a degree of independent action occurred. Where there could be concerted action it was taken but it couldn't be taken too easily. But the need for it was seen and, as I said, James Gordon Finlayson was with me in the Western Desert and he saw it and got into the Tactical Division at the Air Ministry and started to plot it out. Everybody realised it had to be done and gradually it was done. But once a small campaign in a particular area is completed, when all things have come together, the whole process starts again in a different campaign because personalities have changed.

There followed a rather fragmented discussion on the extent to which inter-Service co-operation depends upon personalities as opposed to doctrine, the consensus being that the interplay of personalities was of vital significance particularly among those at the top. Among the points mentioned were: the transfer of a considerable number of Army personnel to the RAF after the Battle of Britain and its possible influence; change of uniform more likely meant change of allegiance; nevertheless, all the mutual understanding in the world cannot get over the problem of lack of communications which were initially so lacking in the N African campaign. Led by Prof Bond, two or three speakers frequently raised the bomber offensive issue, its contentious nature and RAF's failure to develop a rival doctrine.

D)

The contribution of 'Y' units was warmly acknowledged by *Sir Frederick Rosier,* as an operational user of Y-derived intelligence. Ideally, 'Y', operational headquarters and associated GCIs and radars were linked by good, reliable communications. He described an example of effective co-operational (monitored also by Aileen Clayton in 'The Enemy is Listening'): "I was told by the 'Y' unit that an attack was building up: Italian Air Force Stukas escorted by Me 109s. Our main airfields were at Gambut but heavy rains had bogged us down and we couldn't operate. The enemy airfields were on higher ground in the Jebel Akdar. I decided it was worthwhile to try to trick the enemy and told our forward radar at Gazala that they would be hearing instructions to which they would respond by saying 'Roger', and no more. This was because the Germans, whom we knew were listening in, might D/F us. Eventually the raid was on its way and I scrambled some imaginary fighters. These were vectored and vectored but I thought it was not going to work because I had said: 'You should see them any moment; they are only 5 to 10 miles away.' All at once there was a triumphant message from 'Y' saying that the Italians had jettisoned their bombs and the Germans were playing hell with them. They were planning to bomb Tobruk. It was a trick one could always try once."

Local locations for the 'Y' service were not always practicable. *Mr Goldberg* said that one location for his unit – 700 metres up in the Medjorda mountains – gave optimum conditions for its main task of intercepting signals traffic from Sardinia and through the Sicilian Channel to the east of Tunisia: "The problem was that we were 22 miles north of the airfield complex at the Souk-el-Arba base of our principal client – 224 Group, commanded by Group Captain K. B. B. Cross. If we had been closer we risked being screened by the mountains to the north. We had to communicate by landline with the 224 Group controller and the natives, having discovered the value of the wire, were constantly dismantling it. Air Formation Signals had an almost permanent job maintaining the line, leading to frequent delays in reporting our intercepts."

Mr Goldberg said: "The German pilots were not very security conscious. Their locations, heights, intentions were very thinly coded. It was just a race against the clock whether the information could be used operationally . . . I never heard any bad language or swearing." He was not aware of any attempt by the enemy to disguise their transmissions. On our side there was jamming and beam bending of enemy transmissions, as well as SIGINT. As regards the overall success of 'Y', Mr Goldberg made no special claim except that it played a useful part in the final victory: "We established the GAF Order of Battle, we knew whom we were facing and exactly where they came from . . . we are credited, in particular, with helping to destroy the German air transport fleet – the 323s and Ju 52s – which first tried to reinforce and supply the Tunisian bridgehead and then to evacuate it."

Mr Talbot Green asked about the closeness of the links between aircraft in the air and, as an example, the Gazala radar mentioned by Sir Fred Rosier, instancing practical experience (described in a book by a GCI controller, John Kemp) which militated against the efficient control of fighter operations. *Sir Fred* confirmed that pilots were not filtered but came through to his HQ where control was exercised: "There was a bit of a timelag." This led to an important discussion of the time factor in making intelligence available to those who needed to use it quickly, and of the optimisation of data, i.e. how to get the right balance between too little and too much. Comparisons were drawn between the desert campaigns of 1941/3 and 1991. *Wg Cdr Chitty* said that in the Gulf War much more information was available in real time, even of target strikes. "The problem for the Commander in the modern air force is that the rate of transmission – both digitalised and by voice – is so vast that his problem is to actually assess the amount of information. The next stop is to produce a Command and Control System which must be able to provide information for accurate tasking, whereas their operational Wing Commander can only have a blinkered view of what his objective is. He cannot see the wide perspective of the battlefield, and this is where we have a problem. The data transfer is so vast and instantaneous that a Commander, with the overhead projectors and blackboard displays currently available, cannot really pick up the detail he needs. In fact, some of the range control systems provide better detail for the Range Controller than will normally be seen in a Command HQ."

Sqdn Ldr Roger Bennett, from his experienced as a Tornado navigator in the Gulf campaign, considered that both for security reasons and to avoid saturating the minds of the aircrews, the "need to know" principle was applied in the interest of successfully executing the specified operational task. He asked *Sir Fred Rosier* what general information was usually available to aircrew in the Desert Air Force. The answer was, "very little compared with Desert Storm": i.e. location of enemy airfields and landing grounds, concentrations of enemy AA, and where the ground conflict was taking place. *Sqdn Ldr Bennett* said essentially the same applied in Desert Storm and was sufficient. On the other hand, in the experience of *Wg Cdr Chitty,* commanders at the GHQ and AHQ level "were being swamped" with information from aircrews, reconnaissance and other sources. His experience when the Battle Management Group was called in to give advice on air support operations was that too much information was available and that a Star Trek-type perception was required of what was going on. Yet another Desert Storm participant said that General Schwarzkopf's HQ in Riyadh had what was in effect a real time repeater of what was being shown on the screens of AWACS aeroplanes, giving 24-hour coverage of the Eastern, Western and Central regions. "Commanders were able to see in real time where their aircraft were and what they were doing." *Group Captain Batchelor,* commenting on the 'need to know' principle, mentioned his experience as CO of a Special Duties Squadron operating in support of SOE: "Of course, we did not know, nor did we need to know, the object of the exercise." One such operation began with a visit from the Controller of Operations. SOE. "All he could say was that the Germans were after an explosive a thousand times more powerful than anything yet known. Knowing John Corbett very well I said to him, "you ought to take more water with it". Of course, there was no mention of heavy water and no mention of atomic or nuclear fission. But this [operation] was the destruction of the Norsk hydroelectric plant in Southern Norway, which was done very successfully. The Germans panicked and shipped the regional stocks to Germany. This stopped them in their tracks and, as we now know, they realised that it would take too long to produce a nuclear weapon. It was not until after the war that we learned what was at stake in the dropping of the team." In Bomber Command there were several things that crews 'needed to know': target maps, obviously, but also security of radar aids – Gee sets were fitted with explosive charges. *Group Captain Batchelor* accepted that there could be good reasons why the current generation of aircrew needed to know more of 'the reason why'. On the other hand, a Wellington pilot from the wartime mediterranean theatre (*Sqn Ldr Cooling*) thought that his own squadron could have been better informed of the broad picture: "We were little more than errand boys . . . there's your aeroplane, there's your bomb load, there's your target; off you go. God willing, you come back and off you go again. But we did begin to discern patterns of operations. Just before the big push that threw the Afrika Korps out of Africa there were presumably quite a number of convoys coming into Algiers and other North African ports to build up the 1st Army. We started to find a pattern of operations in which we used to sit over the airfields of southern Sardinia – three of them – and these were the bases for torpedo bombers, Heinkels, Cants and so forth. A Wimpey couldn't go over there in daylight to stop them taking off, so we sat over those airfields in the dark, wandering around, one aircraft at a time. You had sixteen 250lb. bombs and every time you saw a glimmer of light you dropped one . . . When your hour was up you went home and on the way you dropped one on Elmas which was the airfield the Italians were fairly sensitive about; it had a runway. And that was the signal for the next chap coming up. We did this, day in, day out . . . and I feel that if we had known a little more of the overall picture it would have made more sense and people wouldn't have thought – "milk run again; over there; pull the tit; come back again." *Flight Lieutenant Graham Edwards* thought it unrealistic to expect that in a long drawn out war you could possibly hope to know what you were doing on every mission. He doubted whether knowing the fuller picture would have made any difference to either enthusiasm or effectiveness. *Vincent Orange:* "Clearly we couldn't be told by the top brass that we were going to have an invasion of Sicily in 10 or 12 days, in case were were shot down and captured . . . but WWII commanders, certainly Tedder and Coningham, were better than those of WWI at going round and 'sitting on the sand'. They had been the battle pilots of 1917 and they said they had never been told enough about what they were supposed to be doing. Even Tedder, when he became Eisenhower's deputy in Europe, found he could not get out and about to the same extent." *Wg Cdr Richard Williams*, who was at JHQ during the Gulf War, said that Air Chief Marshal Paddy Hine got out to every operational station in the period immediately before the war began. *Sir Frederick Rosier:* "This helps tremendously. I was a young chap, 26, when I took over a Wing in the desert. In the early days the communication between myself, Bing Cross and 'Mary' Coningham was over radio. We had some American sets, bought off the shelf in Cairo, and we were able to talk to each other in the evenings; all extremely personal. Tedder used to come up quite often, and we had the most marvellous evenings. Tedder was great fun." *Wing Cdr Roger Bennett:* "One significant difference is the effect of the media. We were getting a lot of our intelligence from CNN!" *Sir Frederick Rosier:* "I was horrified and thought it was all wrong. I went up to Leuchars shortly afterwards and was told that the wives left behind there used to assemble at six in the evening and were briefed direct from Dahran about all that had been going on during the day. I was told it was a great comfort to them. Different times, different methods; but the media – well!"

The Crucial Importance of Malta. If the Germans had captured Malta we 'could not have been surprised if Rommel had got into Egypt and swept us all out" (Rosier). Members of the syndicate vied with one another in bringing out various aspects of Malta's importance: as a 'Y' station (Goldberg and Orange), as a base for attacks on enemy supply ships (by submarines and aircraft), as a staging post (as *Ralph Fellows,* a wartime Wellington pilot, testified – "much more difficult to have got replacement Wellingtons to the Far East, as well as the Middle East, without Malta"), and not least as a symbol of resistance against all the odds. With hindsight, the best time for the Axis to have seized Malta was the summer of 1940. Later, there was a plan – Plan Hercules – to invade the island; and a good time would have been around June 1942 after the Allied defeat up at Gazala and the loss of Tobruk. "Rommel, Kesselring and Raeder pressed Hitler to 'liquidate Malta and were home and dry' " (*Sqdn Ldr Cooling*). In air power terms, there would seem to have been a good chance of success: typically, the Malta fighter force would begin the day with 20 aircraft and finish with only 10, or even 5, serviceable; whereas the enemy had 200/300 aircraft available in Sicily. *Wg Cdr Williams* said the German Navy "was not prepared to sanction amphibious operations against Malta, nor was the German Air Force, after Crete, prepared to sanction airborne operations unless air superiority was achieved over the island." This was never achieved. As well as continuing, if hard-pressed, fighter defences, Malta's AA defences were formidable as were its coastal defence guns, which were well dug in. These considerations, after the heavy losses of specialised troops and transport aircraft in the Crete invasions, may have swayed the argument in 1942, with the resources consumed by Barbarossa another major factor. The irony, according to *Vincent Orange,* is that staff colleges and staff officers "are supposed to exist to answer questions such as, 'is the risk of casualties in a particular operation worth taking?' From the German point of view Malta *was* worth heavy casualties, more so than Crete which the Germans took at great expense and then made no particular use of it." *Sqdn Ldr Brown* (Staff college student): "Malta exemplifies the disproportional effect possible from a small number of dedicated weapons: in Malta's case, notably the submarines. Similarly, in the Gulf War, if Iraq had had one conventional submarine there could have been no maritime air power in the Gulf of Hormuz."

The Takoradi-Cairo air supply route was obviously crucial: anecdotally to *Sir Fred Rosier* since it enabled him to withstand the wiles of Hugh Pugh-Lloyd when AOC Malta; "I had flown off a carrier to Malta and was invited to dinner with Hugh Pugh-Lloyd. He plied me with drink and asked, would I mind staying in Malta? I got away with it, pretty early in the morning; I said I couldn't guarantee that my squadron would be much use to him because my best chaps had gone out via Takoradi and would be lost to him. This seemed to clinch it and he let me go." More seriously, *Sir Fred* said that "had the route not been available we would have been lost. It would have taken months for men and supplies to come round via the Cape." Construction and maintenance of the route involved immense effort, and flying conditions were frequently difficult and dangerous (even now, as a Nigerian student at the Staff College testified). Air Cdr. H. K. Thorold (mentioned in Humphrey Wynn's morning address) AOC at Takoradi, was "one of the outstanding heroes of the Mediterranean campaign" (*Vincent Orange*). Dr Orange said that the Cairo to Khano route had been pioneered in the 1920s by none other than 'Mary' Coningham and another officer, flying unsophisticated DHGAs (voice from the floor: "Easier to maintain").

The Takoradi route was a means of supply between the UK and US and the base depots and maintenance units in Egypt. *Desmond Goch* (RAF Hist S.) asked about the problems of supply that arose between the supply depots in Egypt and the squadrons in the desert in what was frequently a fast-moving campaign. Essentially the same question was posed by *Wg Cdr Chitty,* who asked how command and control stood up to the pressures during the retreat to Alamein. During the Gulf War "we were losing small pockets of support and the vast amount of movement swamped our command and control system." *Sir Fred:* "It stood up well because we were falling back on our support organisation; so different from an advance . . . unserviceable aeroplanes were towed back and we stopped at intervals to pour water on the axles. We actually finished that retreat with more aircraft than we started with, thanks to the rapid turn-around of aircraft at the Canal Zone bases, plus those we brought back." *Sir Fred* paid tribute to Group Captain Guy Carter who took over his Group from Bing Cross at a critical time: "He was an old man – turned 40 – but he was marvellous. He had a gift for getting on with people and spent a lot of his time out. I was 2 i/c, doing the ops, and my controllers were also Wing Commanders. [During the retreat] we were able to divide up, so that one lot would go back all ready to control; and as soon as they were ready we would then move back, join up for a short time, and this leap-frog process would continue. It was an incredible feat. Guy Carter had almost no sleep; how he did it, I do not know. I got about 3 hours sleep each 24 hours." Some references between then and now emerged. *Sqdn Ldr Williams:* "Passing instructions in a fluid movement situation, when there must have been chaos to some extent, did you use wireless?" *Sir Fred:* "Yes." *Williams:* "No written confirmation?" *Sir Fred:* "No." *Williams:* "We found in the Gulf that it was often easier to pick up a telephone and speak to someone, especially if you were on Christian name terms. Even if it was not on a secure net, you could talk about all sorts of things, even highly classified, on a personal basis. The problem comes when there is misunderstanding as there can be in a situation where squadrons and enormous amounts of kit are moving around. If something passed verbally was important you had to have something on the record, on a screen or a piece of paper, to remind you or the guy who comes on shift at midnight what you decided at 8 o'clock that morning." *Sir Fred:* "Perhaps ours was simple stuff: communication ground to air was VHF and there could be no misunderstanding there because our retreat was almost a rout, with M/T going back so close (thank God the other side weren't doing much about it) that identification of our own units was easy. Ground-to-ground communications depended on how quick the Air Formation Signals were in putting in landlines. They were magnificent; linked to us and with us all the time. They would lay landlines rapidly to these little patches of airfields; otherwise, communication had to be by radio. Nothing written; all done by word of mouth. No question of handling over. We were there; at the double!"

Tony Jones (RAF Hist.S.) asked about the relative quality of aircraft. The Desert Air Force seemed to have had "a rag-bag of types, including lend-lease aircraft," not well suited to such a hostile environment. *Sir Fred:* "The enemy had Macchi 200s and 202s, Stukas, Me 110s and 109s. We had mainly Hurricanes, Tomahawks and Kittyhawks. The Navy had one squadron of fighters (at the beginning in November 1941) with a variety of aeroplanes such as the Grumman Martlet. Overall, we were not bad against the 110 but were markedly inferior to the 109. In the desert the Hurricanes had to be fitted with Vokes filters which downgraded their performance somewhat. At first Kittyhawks had to change engines about every 20 hours because of sand ingestion . . . and until they were fitted with filters things were pretty bad." *Gp Capt Batchelor:* "So often we seem to have to relearn our lessons. Squadrons came out to the Middle East, during the pre-war Abyssinian crisis, without filters and got into trouble. It is no fun flying in dust storms. One of his squadron made 18 forced landings on one flight. History seems to have repeated itself during the Gulf War when, so he understood, dust had the effect of siliconing Tornado turbine blades." *Sir Fred:* "The dust storms were terrible and the more so because the movement of tanks and trucks broke the surface. Often all a pilot could do was force-land and wait. This was easier for the Tomahawks and Kittyhawks because they had internal batteries. It was said that, among the Bedouin, after two days of Khamsin murder was accepted."

Both the strategic and tactical objective was to gain air superiority. *Sir Fred:* "We were determined to continue this fight . . . in some ways it grated a lot because in doing so our casualties were quite high. We did it by sending out sweeps and also by ground attacks, which meant straffing airfields. On meeting the 109s almost straightaway we were forced into defence circles. Now that has been criticised by certain people in books I've read; it's been said that the desert pilots were not as well trained and expert as those in the UK. This was not the point. The Me 109s with their better performance could attack when they wanted to and go away when they wanted to, whereas we had not got that ability. Nevertheless, in spite of this, we continued; and it had a lot to do with our ground straffing of airfields that, overall, we got air superiority."

Miss Ward (Army Historical Branch): "The BEF fell flat in France and was outfought by the Germans because of their all-arms co-ordination. This stunned us. But did we do much better in the desert? Air Marshal Cross had said that the Air should tell the Army what it would do to help them which seems as daft as the Army telling the Air what is should do without understanding the difficulties. We do seem to learn our lessons the hard way. What about co-operation now?"

Chairman: "We spend 10 months at Bracknell banging each others' heads together about the importance of land/air co-operation."

A suitable note on which to end the discussion of this particular syndicate.

E)

Gen. Strawson My experience of fighting the Germans was in Italy, but since I have written books about the North African and Italian campaigns.

Humphrey Wynn Instead of going into Bomber Command, as I had expected, I was trained at Kemble to fly several types of aircraft and then sent as a Sgt. pilot to the Middle East via West Africa; we did a quick conversion course and were then sent to fly along the Takoradi route. I was there in 1942-44 on ferry pilot duties – a wonderful opportunity to fly every kind of aircraft.

Peter Rudd I was a pilot with 23 Squadron flying Mosquitoes from Luqa in 1943.

Grp Capt Patrick Foss I joined the RAF in 1932; left the Service in 1938; rejoined 1939; flew Wellingtons. One night I was ordered to take 12 Wellingtons to Malta – 10 of us got there. On arrival we were asked what we were there for. We spent some months chasing the Italian Navy out of ports. Then the Germans joined in the battle, and in four months I lost 40 aircraft, all on the ground. Then I returned to the Air Ministry, put in charge of air reinforcement.

David Nutting I was in technical intelligence and spent three years abroad. I started after Alamein in the Western Desert. We had no transport and nobody wanted to help us. Then we were told to go and count the number of enemy aircraft we had found on a captured German airfield. In the next month we equipped ourselves with enough captured German vehicles, weapons, food, etc., to enable us to follow up the whole offensive through North Africa, Italy and Normandy to Denmark.

Grp Capt Ainsworth Communication between ground and air – when did it actually start to happen, and have we really progressed since, bearing in mind the friendly fire incidents in the Gulf? In World War II the means of doing so entailed several large vehicles and I wonder if we've gone much better.

Gen Strawson Now you have at a lowly level the RAF officer with his vehicle and communications right up with the forward troops – this certainly happened in the Gulf but it didn't in the desert, where the RAF officer was at one of the HQs – so if you wanted air support as a forward operator you had to go back through your own communications to HQ before there could be any response. In Italy we did have RAF representatives up with the leading troops, but at this time the Luftwaffe was not often seen – so it was much easier to call forward the fighters. I well remember that whenever we heard there was an 88 mm round the corner the instant reaction of the troops was to call for a Hurricane.

Nutting I remember seeing an ALO at 30 Corps HQ.

Strawson Yes, we were unlikely to find one at Division HQ. We would hear that one of our Division HQs had been overrun by the Germans – a cheer went up instantly!

Probert John Terraine's book records that the September 1941 Directive issued in North Africa introduced jointly staffed air support HQs at each Corps and Division, and introduced a Forward Air Support link at Brigade level. I believe it worked pretty well, particularly in the later stages at Alam Halfa and El Alamein.

Boog In the German system we had forward squads consisting of an air officer and two or three radio operators, and we had it down to Divisional level. We also had forward operators with radio telephones who gave the Stukas, etc., their targets.

Rudd In Normandy we had the black and white stripes painted on our aircraft.

Probert Bomb lines have always been an anxiety. There were several occasions in Normandy when large formations were wrongly attacked – the Americans lost a full General on one occasion. There is nothing peculiar in what happened in the Gulf and it annoys me intensely when I see the amount of publicity around one little incident and think of the care taken these days. I make the general observation that such incidents are inseparable from the business of modern warfare. Whatever precautions you take these things are going to happen, and what we should be surprised at is that they happened so rarely in the Gulf – a remarkable tribute to those who were there. It occurred far more in WW2 and on a much bigger scale.

Sqdn Ldr Leakey (a ground attack pilot) For all the modern organisation you have, in the heat of the moment in close air support, the problem of communication to the Forward Air Controller, where even now – because you are at very low level – it is very difficult. You have the problem of target acquisition; the particular incident mentioned was a stand-off attack by an A10 with Martel, so he had the visual acquisition problem as well from some distance back. It was the ground attack airman's nightmare. Even when under positive FAC control it is very tough to distinguish between troops dug in and camouflaged and another set of troops. I would like to echo Air Cdre Probert's comments.

Probert General Strawson, would you rather have good quality air support and run the risk of it going wrong or accept that it was going to be so constrained that you would not get an effective level of support?

Strawson Of course, the former – a really effective method of calling for air support which might occasionally go wrong. In the Gulf my own Regiment suffered two men wounded because of an American aircraft firing rockets which hit an APC. There was no question of any Iraqi vehi cles being in that area and there was a great misreading of the situation by the American pilots. In WW2 the RAF's support in the Desert, in Italy and in Normandy was superb. The cab ranks were an enormously reassuring sight, and in difficult country like Italy or parts of Normandy, when getting around the obstacle was almost impossible, the only way to deal with some of these difficult positions was with air power. An RAF officer would be told "there is an 88 mm gun in that farmhouse" and the next moment a Typhoon was shooting it up and you could move on.

John Peaty Much work has been done recently on the work of the Typhoons in Normandy and the claims were greatly overstated. The Typhoons were attacking at great speed and the rockets were unguided. The exaggeration was compounded by the fact that the scale of destruction in the Falaise Gap made it impossible to tell which vehicles had been destroyed by artillery and which by air attack.

Grp Capt Ainsworth I was fascinated to hear that there were FACs running the Stukas well before Alamein. The whole thing hung on whether you could reliably talk from the ground to the pilot within a common frame of reference.

Gen Strawson The whole German tactical doctrine was based on Blitzkrieg, which meant the closest co-operation between Panzer power and air power. So right from the start the winning of a battle depended on the concentrated thrust of air and ground power. So close co-operation between the Luftwaffe and the Wehrmacht was the basis of tactical doctrine.

Boog I must contradict! The Luftwaffe started out to become a strategic bomber force. The Army opposed this concept – it wanted planes to help the infantry get out of the trenches rather than bombing industries in the hinterland. In 1936 the concept changed towards co-operation – smaller bombers. But co-operation was to be indirect; close air support was thought to be impossible. But during the Spanish Civil War this close air support was developed, though there were no proper communications. Then in 1939 the Luftwaffe used close air support for the first time. With the successes in Poland and France it became a close air support force. In Russia even the heavy bombers were used in this way.

Wynn Did not the Luftwaffe have to become a strategic bomber force in the Battle of Britain?

Boog It was a tactical air force used strategically. The original task was to help the Army across a big river (the Channel), for which air superiority was needed in the landing area. But the Luftwaffe officers, wanting to establish their independent role, felt the only way was to conduct an independent air war. So there was no real plan for the strategic air offensive. Only in co-operation, eg in Russia, was the Luftwaffe victorious.

THE END OF THE BEGINNING 85

Strawson The Stuka was essentially a tactical bomber, surely.

Boog The dive bomber concept was originally strategic, and it applied to all bombers, even the four engined ones. This was why the He 177 never became operational. The dive bomber principle had been developed in the Weimar period – the strategic bomber would penetrate the enemy's air space and hit its target by diving.

Strawson I thought the Stuka was regarded as airborne artillery to help the troops forward (*Boog* Yes, it developed into that). Strategic bombing surely didn't have to be as precise as that.

Boog But that is what they *did* think!

Peter Montgomery Coming back to rockets, I found that if the aircraft was trimmed out accurately to fly at rocket-launching speed the accuracy was very good.

Sqdn Ldr Carver Friendly fire incidents were fewer in the Gulf because the technology had come on apace. With the advent of modern navigation systems the ground troops knew where they were, there was better mapping, the aircraft knew where they were. Turning to navigation, I've been in the Middle East in a Hercules, and been grateful for the Nile. What was navigation like for Mr Wynn?

Wynn I was asked to fly a Corsair out in convoy from the UK to the Delta area. We had to refuel at Rennes; I lost the convoy and had to continue on my own. On arriving in the Middle East I was told I should not have flown all this way by myself – yet I'd been doing it for years. If you were asked to fly a new type of aircraft you often did so without benefit of pilot's notes.

Foss In the Air Ministry I was told to advise the PM on the flow of aircraft right through from Takoradi to Cairo. Every week I sent a return. One day a message came "I notice that Hurricane so-and-so has been sitting at Fort Lamy for over a month – when will it move?" I asked Cairo, who had lost it. It has probably been abandoned. Another day we were told the southern route had been closed. Why? The message came back: a Liberator full of American Generals had arrived at one of the landing grounds and asked for gas: they had taken up to 2-3000 gallons and it would take our camels each carrying 4 gallon drums at least a month to replenish!

Wg Cdr Bruce Wynn Air Marshal Dawson was mentioned; how did his role relate to that of Elmhirst?

Wynn Tedder wanted maintenance and repair to be under a high level officer equivalent in rank to SASO and AOA. Previous AOA – AVM Maund – was working through the whole hot Egyptian day trying to keep up. Tedder realised this was not on.

Probert Elmhirst was AOA; remember you did not have the third prong in the main HQ. AOA was trying to do everything that was not connected with air operations.

Wynn The technical work was becoming so much more demanding.

Probert Elmhirst was Tedder's right hand man in sewing up all the aspects of support. Coningham did not have a feel for the minutiae of administration; he needed a good Chief of Staff – this was virtually what Elmhirst did. But behind them they needed the equivalent of what the RAF had back at home – industrial back-up. Aircraft could not be returned to industry for major repairs – everything had to be done out there, and this was the significant achievement. It was the first time we had built up a mini-industrial maintenance organisation to look after all our equipment – repair, maintenance, major servicing, rebuilding, all had to be done locally. This was all brand new. Pre-war when major work was required you either wrote it off or sent it back to the UK. but now you could not do this. No conflict between the tasks of Elmhirst and Dawson; they were complementary.

Wg Cdr Leathart I was staff officer engineering and logistics in Riyadh during Granby – the Dawson equivalent! I am struck by the comparisons between North Africa and Desert Storm. It was a coalition operation, again with the USAF; an RAF force was under American command eventually; its principal objective was land support (having gained air superiority). on the logistics side there are three comparisons: (1) command and control. Dawson apparently was under UK command (not under Tedder) (*Wynn:* No, he was under Tedder – he just did not appear there on the Air Force List, for the Air Ministry did not want to disturb the hierarchy. This was a wartime solution to a desperate problem; Tedder pushed it through despite them.) It is often the case that the logistics provided are insufficient for the operation that develops after contact with the enemy – this was certainly true in the ME, and it was the same in North Africa. Close liaison between the logistics and air commanders is essential. (2) The bomb stores (Air Stores Parks) are difficult to move as a squadron advances – we had this problem with the Harriers, where logistics limit the ability of the air support to advance. (3) The reinforcement route. We had to replace lost Tornados and also needed a reinforcement route – though AAR made it much faster. The squadrons providing close air support (mainly American, apart from Jaguars) did not need to advance in concert with air forces because we had AAR; so AAR influenced speed of reinforcement and increased reach.

Foss Sitting in Air Ministry I saw a different angle – MAP had a "thinking" about how to get things done by bending the rules, but in AM we were very grateful for Dawson – he was a "brigand" – if something needed fixing he fixed it regardless of the paperwork. He had been in

MAP previously and his own links with Beaverbrook, etc., helped him to get things done.

Rudd Not everyone went via Takoradi; 23 Squadron – 18 aircraft – went in 1942 via Gibraltar to Malta. All reinforcements went that way – we could not wait; squadron strength by May was down to 7.

Wynn The role of Gibraltar in aircraft supply is often overlooked. There were also considerable assembly facilities.

Probert Most of the aircraft using the Takoradi route were those which had crossed the Atlantic from the States or aircraft lacking the range to use the Mediterranean route.

AVM Newton How was the Army supplied and reinforced?

Strawson Wavell gets full marks for foreseeing in 1939 the need for a substantial base in the Delta area; he was determined to see the base soundly built up. There was a year or so to do it, so even before the land operations started the ME base was well stocked and the lines of communication (mainly round the Cape) were firmly established. So one started with a logistically solid base. I do not believe the RAF contributed greatly to the build-up of supplies, which was nearly all done by convoys, mainly round the Cape but also several valuable ones – eg Tiger – through the Med. Throughout the campaign the supplies kept coming, via the Red Sea, etc – never were we so pushed for supplies that tactical operations were inhibited. And each time we were pushed back we were that much nearer the main base. Montgomery, of course, was determined not to advance without being absolutely secure logistically.

Probert We should remind ourselves of the constant attack on the Axis supply routes from Italy and Sicily to North Africa, and the significance of Malta. Can Dr Boog contribute?

Boog The fundamental question was whether to take Malta or Cairo. There was an Italian contingency plan before the war to take Malta as a first step in war. This seems to have been forgotten and in 1941 the Germans realised no success was possible without logistics so they decided to take Malta. Hitler, Goering, Kesselring all favoured it, so 2nd Fliegerkorps was placed in Sicily in order to make Malta ripe for invasion. The bombing occurred mainly in March/April 1942, but the timing was not co-ordinated with the intentions of the Italians, who were preparing for an invasion but said in late April that they needed three more months. The Germans had by now planned their second big offensive in Russia and Kesselring – aware how few aircraft, etc, there were in Malta – said he could hold down Malta for the next few. Then Rommel, who had been ordered not to go behind the Libyan border, was so successful that he decided to press on further – and now he had Hitler's support (Hitler did not trust the Italians and he persuaded Mussolini, who had favoured taking Malta). This was the fundamental mistake: Hitler was against taking Malta in the end – he recalled the great losses in Crete. An enormous amount of cargo was being shipped to North Africa, but Malta could not be kept down and more and more ships were being sunk. During the Battle of Alamein four tankers were sunk, which almost immobilised the Afrika Korps. Not talking Malta was the biggest mistake.

Wynn This was the Battle of the Atlantic in reverse. As long as Malta survived it had offensive as well as defensive roles. Its torpedo-carrying aircraft – Beauforts and the FAA – and its submarines attacked the German supply conveyors. This was Malta's role in the Desert War.

Strawson The attack on Crete was so disastrous in the loss of Student's paratroop corps that Hitler said there would be no more parachute ops. And Malta could not have been taken without them. After capture of Tobruk, Rommel felt he had all he needed – but it was not enough to take him to Cairo.

Boog Two more points on Malta. In the summer of 1941, when it seemed Russia would be crushed, a plan was made to destroy the British Empire by going through the Caucasus into Persia and also through North Africa. This opportunity seemed possible again in the summer of 1942. They thought it just might work, but it was an illusion. Another point; since Rommel was not in Egypt he could be supplied via Greece and Crete – stupid, for there was only one railway line.

Sqdn Ldr Chalmers Why did not Germany persuade Spain to have a go at Gibraltar, which would have stopped the convoys, etc?

Boog We tried hard, but Franco was too clever. He depended on grain from Canada; he needed much from the Allied side, and Spain was still suffering from the Civil War. He could not take the risk.

Strawson Admiral Raeder tried to persuade Hitler in early 1941 to take Gibraltar and seize North Africa, for he was convinced the British would try to do this. No shortage of pressure on Hitler, but his eye was on Russia. Secondly, Hitler's comment on Franco: "I'd rather have all my teeth out than another hour with that man."

Foss We too were bringing much pressure on Spain.

Sqdn Ldr Pennington How much intelligence information ex-ULTRA, etc, penetrated to the flying squadrons? Was air recce partly used as a cover? How far was 'Y' information used by us and by the Germans?

Boog Rommel has his 'Y' Service, and we intercepted the messages of the US Military Attache in Cairo. We did not know that the British intercepted our messages – we thought the Italians had betrayed us, giving the British details of our convoys. Since 1975, however, we have known the truth. We did the same with yours!

Foss In Malta in 1941, the AVM told me 250 Italian bombers were sitting on Castel Benito and we ought to go at once to destroy them. We set off at dusk and caught them on the ground and heard next day on Italian 'Y' 109 aircraft had been destroyed or badly damaged. We must have got the original information by 'Y' or 'ULTRA'.

Rudd Aileen Clayton (The Enemy is Listening) refers to occasions when we heard the enemy had cancelled ops because the presence of intruders had grounded the bombers. 23 Squadron specialised in this sort of operation and was so willing to operate on the strength of 'Y' that they became one of our favourite customers. As a squadron pilot I was not aware of 'Y' – we would often sit over an airfield all night and think it a waste of time. I did not need to know. The intelligence briefings we got were fine. The prime purpose was to stop the enemy bombing Malta, and our job was to go out and sit over his airfields. We were also involved in co-operation with the NF Beaufighters (108 Squadron) – we would be sent to stir up trouble over Sicily in the hope they would send up night fighters. A Beaufighter would be waiting at low level under Malta control with 'Y' also listening, waiting for the JU88 to take off. One night I was told to pretend to be a bomber, flying at 160 knots, with a Beaufighter below, waiting – not very pleasant. Once the NF got near us Malta would alert the Beau which would then tackle the JU88. It succeeded once.

Probert Y Service was known about on both sides. Enormous precautions were taken to try to ensure that Ultra information was not used in a way that would indicate that we might be reading Enigma. The initial transcription was done at Bletchley Park and material based on it would go out to the Special Liaison Units in theatre. They then passed it on to the top commanders – very few were in on the secret.

Foss In Malta in the early days we had very little ground support for our first Wellington squadron. When we were ordered to bomb Naples we needed help – an appeal went out and the Navy produced 200 sailors from the Swordfish squadron (at first we were not allowed to talk direct to them!). I had a civilian friend in the Dockyard, and he came up with 200 "mateys", none of whom had worked on aeroplanes and many of whom did not speak English. Now we had a labour force. Then the Germans bombed us plastered us. I spotted an Army Colonel who had come to see what was going on. "How many men have you got?" "About 200." "I have 300 – we will be here in half an hour. You get those aeroplanes in the air; we will fill those holes." And they did! Every time it happened again they were back to fill the holes. They came to load the bombs too. That was a remarkable case of "conversion" – up to then we had been quite separate.

Strawson SAS contribution also deserves recognition. David Stirling and his men destroyed 3-400 aircraft on the ground on the desert airfields.

This was the starting point for the SAS.

Probert How good were the relations between the Luftwaffe commanders and Rommel and his men?

Boog Both HQs were usually close together, but Rommel had no idea about the particular problems of the Luftwaffe. When he was advancing he called for air support but he did not know how long it took to organise the ground facilities. He knew it was important but he moved his troops without reference to the air side.

Wynn Talking of mobility it was not enough to move a squadron to another LG: the fitters too had to be moved, the fuel, the ammo, etc. Not easy either to find the airfields.

Sqdn Ldr Collins How much use was made of the other side's logistics?

Strawson Rommel used to get his petrol from us!

Probert The origins of the RAF Regiment's role in airfield defence are to be found in the Western Desert campaigns – crucial for its history. We had to take on close defence of airfields ourselves.

Wynn On one occasion two Hurricane squadrons operated far behind enemy lines to attack the Afrika Korps while they were retreating. Neil Cameron was involved in this.

F)

Wg Cdr Horwood opened proceedings by asking the participants what it was like to be in-theatre during the Desert War. *Tony Richardson* recalled that it was "pretty bloody". He said that he served as a sgt air gunner on a Wellington sqn towards the end of the desert campaign, and he commented that morale, amongst ground crews, was not high. Regulars who had been out in the desert for a prolonged period just wanted to go home. He remembered that conditions were poor; the sqn lived in tents, there were no beds and the food was basic — "sand in everything". He remarked that sqn personnel were a mix of Britons, Australians and Canadians, sgt aircrew mainly. His overwhelming feeling was that people just wanted to get on with the job, finish the tour and go home. Operations consisted predominantly of the Bengahzi "mail run" and some raids on Heraklion, though his sqn was also involved in daylight low-level ops on transport targets during the retreat to El Alamein. He also mentioned that leave periods in Cairo were not always wonderful. *Mr Cullum* did not agree with this picture, especially over morale. He had deployed with 37 Sqn in late 1940, and he felt that on his unit, a constituted sqn, morale was very high, with a good rapport between air and ground crew. Conditions he thought had been quite acceptable — Fayid and Shalufah were not unlike wartime stations at home. Food was poor, but the diet was supplemented by fresh fruit flown in from Israel. He said that conditions at the Forward Landing Grounds (FLGs) were primitive but acceptable, though he agreed that sand was always a problem. *Brig Routledge*, referring to morale, commented that there was a world of difference between the morale of fighting troops and the personnel in the rear areas. He remarked that fighting units accepted setbacks stoically, whereas real panic sometimes broke out amongst the staffs in Cairo. *Tony Richardson* then qualified his remarks on morale, explaining that rather than describe it as poor, it would be fairer to say that in his experience, personnel indulged in the time-honoured British tradition of "binding and griping" about conditions.

Mr Cullum said that his sqn also operated in Greece from Tatoi (Melindi) and he said that conditions here were reasonable. He stressed the benefits of deploying as a formed unit — in his sqn, the combination of regular officers and VR personnel resulted in the maintenance of sensible discipline. He also remarked that the early operations against the Italians were relatively easy, with few losses, even in Greece. Targets in the desert were easy to find, despite the lack of aids. and defences were poor. Ops were more difficult in Greece; the terrain was mountainous and there were no aids, with navigation by map and DR. He recalled an operation to Tirana in Albania when his sqn was tasked to bomb a house where Mussolini was supposed to be staying. His captain made 6 attacks from 2000 ft, dropping 2 bombs each time, but with no particular success.

Wg Cdr McPhee noted that crews in the Gulf War had not deployed as complete sqns and drew an analogy with the RAF experience of 50 yrs previously. He asked what was the best method; formed sqns or individual crews? *Mr Cullum* was convinced that it was much better to deploy as a complete sqn, but he acknowledged that most crews did not move as part of constituted sqns. *Mr Richardson* said that ex-OTU crews ferried out new aircraft and then went into a holding pool until allocated to a sqn — 108 sqn in his case. He mentioned that most bombers deployed through the Mediterranean; the Takoradi route was used mainly for fighters. *Wg Cdr Trigg* said that he had been SEngO of 101 Sqn in the Gulf War, and he felt that deployment as a complete sqn was the best way. He then asked how POWs were dealt with in the fluid operations that characterised the Desert War. *Brig Routledge* recalled that there were a series of transit and holding camps that collected and funnelled POWs from the point of capture back to the eventual permanent camps in the UK or Canada.

The discussion on POWs led *Mr Thomas* to mention the sinking of a British ship carrying 1800 Italian POWs by a U-boat, and the subsequent attempts by other U-boats to effect a rescue. He also commented upon the implications of intelligence work on the situation when 350,000 POWs had to be cared for after the Axis surrender at Cape Bon in 1943. The success of the allied code-breakers meant that the Allies had a great deal of information on Axis' shipping movements, cargoes, routes and escorts. and this allowed a degree of discrimination in targeting — food ships could be allowed in whilst tankers could be sunk by the Malta-based Wellingtons and submarines. In this way, the DAK was starved of fuel, but sufficient food was accumulated which was later used to feed the Axis POWs. He expounded further on the success of Ultra. After Rommel had been forced to break off the Crusader battle because of lack of fuel, attempts were made to subjugate Malta, by extra U-boats and the deployment of Flieger Korps 10 to Sicily. The 6 month respite thus gained allowed Rommel to advance to the Alamein line. However, Ultra gave details of fuel convoy moves, allowing these to be attacked, and Flieger Korps 10 was forced to abandon its attacks on the Delta to give cover to the convoys. Ultra gave Tedder knowledge of this switch and allowed him to strip the Delta of fighter cover in order to protect the 8th Army.

Wg Cdr Horwood asked for a re-assessment of Montgomery's role. *Brig Routledge* said that he felt that Montgomery's greatest strength was his innate caution. He rarely took any risks, only attacking when he had significant superiority in men and materiel; his besetting sin was that he always believed he was right. He said that Montgomery was a luckier general than Wavell, and much more ruthless with failure. *Mr Thomas* mentioned that Montgomery took over just before Alam Halfa, and that Ultra gave him warning of the impending attack. Montgomery was thus able to take credit for prescience in foiling the attack, whilst Rommel blamed the Italians for giving the game away. Wg *Cdr Crichton* asked whether Rommel suspected that Enigma had been compromised, as he thought it was incredible that the Germans should have maintained such blind faith in the system. *Mr Thomas* said that the Germans did keep their faith in Enigma, preferring to suspect other forms of compromise. including treason — thus illustrating the mind-set of totalitarian regimes.

Wg Cdr Crichton then asked about the development of Army-RAF cooperation and the influence of Broadhirst. *Mr Thomas* gave much of the credit for the emergency of a joint HQ to Ultra. Apparently, Bletchley Park could read Flieger Fuehrer Afrika's daily signals on aircraft states and the general operational situation, and it was the dissemination and use of this intelligence data that spurred the development of joint HQs; in his view therefore, Ultra was very important in unifying the Services. *Mr Shores* said that Broadhirst arrived in Cairo in late summer '42 and was available to command the Desert Air Force (DAF) in time to mastermind the fighter-bomber attacks that were so vital to the breaching of the Mareth Line in March 1943. In effect, he refined the Coningham system and maintained very close liaison with the Army. *Mr Thomas* commented that Broadhurst was very receptive to Ultra information. *Brig Routledge* thought that the improvement in Army/Air co-operation owed much to improved technology, especially in communications, allowing the development of a forward air controller system (FAC) that reached its apogee in Normandy. *Wg Cdr Crichton* mentioned the Cassino battles in Italy, and the effectiveness of the jeep-mounted FACs. *Lt Col Palomeros* asked how the Germans conducted their air/land battle management. *Mr Shores* said that they used a different system. German fighters were allocated a "frei jagd" role to clear the air of allied aircraft to allow their bombers to operate unmolested; tactical aircraft like the Ju 87s and the fighter-bombers were more closely controlled, more along the lines of the DAF. *Maj Seebei* raised the question of targeting policy, asking who chose the targets, the army or air?' *Mr Shores* explained that targeting policy and priorities changed as the joint command system evolved — the greater the degree of army/air co-operation, the greater say the army had in targetting, particularly from mid-42 onwards.

Maj Marsh mentioned that the RAF jammed Rommel's communications and he asked who had made that decision. *Brig Routledge* said that comms jamming was an RAF initiative from the outset, and *Mr Thomas* confirmed that jamming formed part of the overall deception plan to mislead Rommel about allied intentions.

Gp Capt Neubroch posed a seminal question when he asked "What was the key to success in land/air operations?". The question was not properly answered, though *Mr Shores* expanded on Vincent Orange's thesis on the Montgomery/Coningham partnership. Various speakers felt that success came via a number of incremental steps, until the cab-rank system that was to dominate the Normandy battlefield eventually evolved.

G)

Air Cdre Rainsford described his task as CO of a Wellington sqn., one of four in the Middle East. Nearly all operations were directed against Benghazi, or occasionally Derna or Bardia, in an attempt to disrupt the German supply lines. Generally the aircraft flew with a full bombload from Kabrit to a forward landing ground to take on more fuel, before taking off again for the target. The Wellingtons also became involved in the campaign in Greece, where they bombed and mined the Corinth Canal, which was the only occasion that he experienced flak being fired downwards at his aircraft from clifftops overhead.

Wg Cdr Lucas described his experiences as a Flight and Squadron commander on Malta. He found it surprising that the only person in the morning session to mention the crucial importance of Malta to our position in North Africa had been an Army general. Malta's effectiveness in disrupting Rommel's supply lines had been crucial to the victories in the Desert. He thought in particular that recognition should be given to the quality of the intelligence which made the attacks on Axis convoys so successful.

Lt Col Mark Wells USAF asked whether there had been any problem with operational fatigue or morale on squadrons in the Middle East.

Air Cdre Rainsford replied that his squadron had been at Kabrit, and that there were therefore opportunities for people to get to Ismailia and Cairo, where there was some social life. Up in the Western Desert it was rather different, but on the whole morale had been very good. The most important factor in maintaining morale was the regular arrival of mail which had generally been achieved. The only time he felt the morale in his squadron deteriorated was when the rations started to include Egyptian sweet potatoes instead of ordinary potatoes, and it reached its nadir when rice replaced the sweet potatoes!

Wg Cdr Lucas thought that morale was more of a problem on multi-engined squadrons than on single-engined fighters. In his three operational tours he did not see any instance of LMF, but he regarded it as the job of the Sqn. Commander to detect the signs of stress early and take appropriate action.

Group Captain Hugh Verity said he had not experienced the problem on any of his squadrons, but that he had once visited a friend's Blenheim squadron in No 2 Group which was engaged on anti-shipping operations. The loss rate was one aircraft per 4 sorties, and in that squadron early morning tea was not tea but beer. His friend rose from Flying Officer to Wing Commander in six months.

Lt Col Wells Asked whether fighter and bomber pilots tended to be different personalities.

Wg Cdr Lucas thought the temperament required to undertake missions to Schweinfurt as a B-17 pilot, was certainly not that normally found in a Spitfire pilot.

Wg Cdr Statham asked about inter-service relations.

AVM Stapleton said that relations between the RAF and the RN were poor largely because it was very difficult for the RAF in North Africa, and the RN at sea in the Mediterranean, to form a close understanding of the other service's work. This remoteness often militated against closer co-operation. Co-operation with the Army eventually became very close, largely, he believed, because of the work of Mary Coningham, who ensured that units from each service lived and worked in close proximity. In 1939, however, he recalled having to communicate with Army units by means of handwritten messages attached to flags and dropped from the aircraft, i.e. there had been no discernible advance since the First World War.

Mr Cox pointed out that part of the reason for the lack of sophisticated techniques of army co-operation lay in the fact that, until March 1939, the British Government had only agreed to a VERY small scale commitment of troops to a continental war, and in those circumstances it was unsurprising that the RAF had done so little. When the Government performed a *volte face* and agreed to send a large scale force to the Continent the Air Staff began to write minutes indicating that they would have to take army co-operation rather more seriously. As all the industrial planning of the previous five years had been based on the assumption of a small scale army co-operation requirement it was no simple matter to alter the priorities at a late stage.

9. Closing Address

Air Chief Marshal Sir Michael Armitage

It falls to my lot to offer some concluding thoughts at the end of a fascinating day. I have managed to look briefly on all the discussion groups and to gain some feel for what people have found particularly interesting. I have heard, for example, of the importance of logistics, with that long and complicated trail across Central Africa and the oceans beyond in order to supply the Middle East. The importance of Malta also came up both to the Armies in North Africa and vice versa. Doctrine was discussed, with the stultifying effect it had on operations, particularly during the first two wartime years. Whatever happened to flexibility in air power thinking? Above all the subject of communications came up, the flow of information — including intelligence, which was also stressed — and extending to communications in the form of cooperation between commanders (RAF/Army, RAF/Navy, RAF/USAAF).

If John Terraine will permit, let me return to the Battle of Amiens which he mentioned this morning, just to illustrate how bad things were only three months before the end of World War 1. Over the battlefields at that time, when the use of aircraft had somewhat matured, the RAF squadrons had four roles. One was reconnaissance, coupled with the crucial ability to make adequate maps. The second was the artillery patrol, tasked to identify enemy artillery positions and direct counter-battery fire against them. The third was the counter-attack patrol designed to look for groups of enemy forces preparing to launch counter-attacks against our own troops. Fourth — and this is a most interesting function of tactical air forces in those days in the context of today's symposium — there were contact patrols. These were to report the position of our own forces on the ground, for once troops advanced towards the enemy positions communications on the ground nearly always broke down. Telephone lines were cut, runners did not get through, the smoke of battle — the smokescreens themselves — added to a general confusion in which brigades and even battalion HQs often did not know what was going on just ahead of them. Contact patrols were meant to fill this gap — such aircraft flew streamers from the biplane struts so that the troops on the ground knew what they were doing. When the crew of the aircraft wished the troops to identify themselves as friendly the crew would sound a klaxon and the troops were expected to identify themselves — eg with coloured discs or flares or even specially issued signalling panels. Sometimes, lacking all else, our troops would lay rifles on the parapet of a captured trench and in line with the trench so that the spotters could see it was occupied by friendly troops. Unfortunately all these signalling devices were equally visible to the enemy, and instead of friendly artillery fire being called down ahead of our troops it was often called down directly onto their positions from enemy guns. As we have heard today, wireless was there in the later stages of the war but only available from air to ground, and even then the messages had to pass through a central information bureau — this took time, and events often overtook the administrative process of handling the messages, allocating units to tasks, and then taking action.

Even when our aircraft might have made a significant contribution against unmistakable targets on or near the battlefield another problem arose. A clear example was the attempt to bomb the bridges over the River Somme, but the heaviest bombs available were only 112lbs — not enough to bring down a bridge, even with a direct hit. During this battle nine RAF squadrons dropped 1563 small bombs and fired a quarter of a million rounds of ammunition from the air, but this must be compared with the artillery effort available some 2000 guns were lined up — one to every eleven yards of front. I make the point that poor communications together with sheer lack of weight meant that the importance of air weapons was minimal when compared with the key role of the artillery. It is this that helps explain the neglect of air/land cooperation between the wars. One result was that the only aircraft specifically procured for the role of land/air cooperation between the wars was the Lysander, built to a specification drawn up in 1934 for a reconnaissance and artillery spotting aircraft. It came into service only in 1938.

As we have seen, very little was done between the wars; here I offer just one thought. For Britain the theatre of war we have been discussing today was very important but for the Germans, once they were engaged on the Eastern Front, it was a sideshow. We were never going to defeat Germany in North Africa. But had we not fought there and had the opportunity to develop and perfect the very good system of air/land cooperation of those days — had we not had that rehearsal — what would have happened in Normandy in 1944? That was the significance of the North African campaign. One of the course members asked today how we could possibly avoid losing important lessons like that again in the future. The answer is that we have days like this.

10. Closing Remarks

Deputy Commandant Air Commodore R. H. Gould

I should like to say thank you on behalf of the Staff College and 84 Advanced Staff Course in particular for what I predicted would be an excellent day and has, in fact, turned out so to be. It has made a splendid contribution to the Air Power Studies phase, and I thank you not only for this morning's excellent presentations but also the stimulating discussions this afternoon.

Air Marshal Sir Frederick Sowrey, Chairman of the RAF Historical Society

Today would not be possible without Bracknell. It is the Commandant, Deputy Commandant and staff who have made it all possible. This morning's presentations interlocked remarkably well, making a fine contribution to RAF history and particularly its poetry. This afternoon we had a lively series of discussions, adding weight to the earlier presentations and we thank Sir Michael Armitage for his chairmanship and succinct comments and summing up. To the members of the Advanced Staff Course we were once you. We hope today has given you a feel for RAF history. Our Historical Society attempts not only to study RAF history but to show that there is relevance between the past and present. You will not be consciously aware of this in your future Service jobs but hopefully you will absorb some of this. Remember that you will be around when we are gone!

Biographical Notes on the Main Speakers

Air Chief Marshal Sir Michael Armitage, KCB, CBE

Air Chief Marshal Mike Armitage joined the RAF in 1947. After service with No 28 Fighter Squadron in Hong Kong, he returned to the UK for 3 tours in Flying Training Command before attending the RAF Staff College in 1965. After a tour as PSO to CinC RAF Germany he commanded No 17 Reconnaissance Squadron at Wildenrath, flying Canberra PR7s. Following the ISSC Course in 1970, he then joined the staff of that establishment before commanding RAF Luqa, in Malta, from 1972 to 1974.

After completing the 1975 RCDS Course, he served for two years as Director of Forward Policy in MOD (Air) before going to RAF Germany as Deputy Commander. Further appointments included Directing Staff at the RCDS and Director of Service Intelligence before becoming the first Chief of Defence Intelligence in 1983; in the same year he was appointed KCB. He then became Air Member for Supply and Organization before completing his final tour in the Royal Air Force as Commandant of the RCDS. He retired in 1990.

Sir Michael is a member of the RUSI and IISS. He contributes to professional journals, and is co-author of the book 'Air Power in the Nuclear Age' published by MacMillan and by the University of Illiniois in 1984 and again in 1985.

Mr John Terraine FRHistS

John Terraine was born in London in 1921 and educated at Stamford School and Keble College, Oxford. He joined the BBC in 1944 as a Recorded Programmes Assistant and did a variety of work including production of Radio Newsreel, programme assistant in the East European Service, and programme organizer of the Pacific and South African service. In 1963 he became associate producer and scriptwriter of the BBC Television series 'The Great War', for which he received the Screenwriters' Guild Documentary Award. He left the BBC in 1964 and scripted 'The Life and Times of Lord Mountbatten' for Thames Television in 1966. In 1974 he was scriptwriter and narrator of the BBC series 'The Mighty Continent'.

He is the author of many books including ten titles about the First World War, and is also the founding President of the Western Front Association. His other books include a biography of Lord Mountbatten, The Mighty Continent and his most recent work, Business in Great Waters, which is a study of the U-boat campaigns in both World Wars. In 1985 he wrote The Right of the Line, a major new study of the RAF's part in the Second World War, and now a standard text on the subject.

In 1982, to mark his contribution to military history, John Terraine received the Chesney Gold Medal, the highest award of the Royal United Services Institute for Defence Studies. In 1987 he became a Fellow of the Royal Historical Society.

Major General John Strawson, CB, OBE

Major General John Strawson served in the 4th Hussars, Winston Churchill's Regiment, during the last war and saw service in the Middle East and Italy. He then took part in various internal security campaigns, including Borneo, when he commanded his Regiment, by then The Queen's Royal Irish Hussars. Later he commanded an infantry brigade and was Chief of Staff UKLF. From 1976 to 1985, he was Military Adviser, Westland Group. He has written several books on military history.

Mr Humphrey Wynn

Humphrey Wynn is a retired Air Historical Branch historian at present working there as a consultant on a history of Transport Command.

His history of the RAF Strategic Nuclear Deterrent Forces was published last year on a Restricted basis, and he had previously written a history of the Post-War Bomber Role.

Before joining the AHB in 1971, he was Deputy Editor and Defence Correspondent of the aviation magazine Flight International.

He served in the RAF 1940-46 as a pilot and in the RAFVR from 1948 to 1980. During his Middle East service, he flew for nine months in 1942-43 on the West African Reinforcement Route to which he will be referring in his contribution to this Symposium.

Air Chief Marshal Sir Frederick Rosier

Air Chief Marshal Sir Frederick Rosier was commissioned in 1935 and posted to No 43(F) Sqn in 1936. In WW2, he saw action in France, UK and the Western Desert. Returning to the UK, he became Station Commander Aston Down (52 OTU) and then Northolt before going to No 84 Gp as Gp Capt Ops and later SASO.

After the war, he had various Command and Staff appointments in UK and USA before going to IDC in 1957. Then came Director of Ex Prospect, D of Plans RAF and Chairman of the JP Committee. After Aug '61 his appointments were AOC Air Force Middle East, SASO Transport Command, AOCinC Fighter Command, UK Military Delegate to CENTO and Deputy CinC Allied Forces Central Europe.

Air Chief Marshal Sir Kenneth Cross, KCB, CBE, DSO, DFC

Air Chief Marshal Sir Kenneth Cross joined the RAF in 1930. After a first tour on 25(F) Squadron, he served first as a flying instructor and then an 11 Gp staff officer before becoming a squadron commander in 1939 and seeing operational service in England, France and Norway. After a brief period as a 12 Gp controller, he moved to the Middle East in 1941 to run the Desert Air Force Fighter Wing and AOC Air Defence Group before becoming AOC 242 Group in 1942, first in Tunisia and subsequently in Sicily and Italy. On returning to the UK in 1944, he served first as Air Commodore Training at HQ AEAF before becoming Director Overseas/Tactical Operations at the Air Ministry.

During his post-war career, and after completing a course at the Imperial Defence College, Sir Kenneth undertook tours in Germany, Fighter Command and the Air Ministry before moving to Bomber Command as a Group Commander. He then became Commander in Chief Bomber Command before moving to become Commander in Chief Transport Command, the post from which he retired in 1968.

Dr Vincent Orange

Dr Orange was born in Shildon, County Durham in 1935 and educated at St. Mary's Grammar School, Darlington, and Hull University, where he gained a PhD. In 1962 he went to live in New Zealand and took up a post as lecturer in history at the University of Canterbury in Christchurch.

His varied career has included 3 years in the RAF and, as an actor, taking part in over 70 radio and stage plays; more recently he has regularly broadcast on a wide range of subjects. He has lectured many times to the New Zealand branches of the Royal Aeronautical Society (to which he was elected an Associate in 1980) and has published several articles on air battles of the Second World War.

His biography of Air Chief Marshal Sir Keith Park was published in 1984 and was follow by a biography of Wing Commander Johnny Checketts, a personal friend and one of New Zealand's best known fighter pilots. His latest work is a biography of another New Zealand airman, Air Marshal Sir Arthur Coningham, which was published in 1990.

Royal Air Force Historical Society

The Royal Air Force has been in existence for more than seventy years; the study of its history is deepening, and continues to be the subject of published works of consequence. Fresh attention is being given to the strategic assumptions under which military air power was first created and which largely determined policy and operations in both World Wars, the inter-war period, and in the era of Cold War tension. Material dealing with post-war history is now becoming available for study under the thirty-year rule. These studies are important both to academic historians and to the present and future members of the RAF.

The RAF Historical Society was formed in 1986 to provide a focus for interest in the history of the RAF. It does so by providing a setting for lectures and seminars in which those interested in the history of the RAF have the opportunity to meet those who participated in the evolution and implementation of policy. The Society believes that these events make an important contribution to the permanent record.

The Society normally holds three lectures or seminars a year in or near London, with occasional events in other parts of the country. Transcripts of lectures and seminars are published in the Proceedings of the RAF Historical Society, which is provided free of charge to members. Individual membership is open to all with an interest in RAF history, whether or not they were in the Service. Although the Society has the approval of the Air Force Board, it is entirely self-financing.

Membership of the Society costs £15 per annum and further details may be obtained from the Membership Secretary, Commander Peter Montgomery, 26 Shirley Drive, Worthing, West Sussex BN14 9AY.

Printed with the generous assistance of

Hastings Printing Company Limited

and

Air Pictorial International